ADVANCE Pɪ ‖‖‖‖‖‖‖‖‖‖‖
KISSING TH T0165813

"Kara Martinez Bachman is hip and funny as hell. If I didn't already have a mother—and if I wasn't nearing middle-age myself—I would ask her to adopt me. I still might ask her."
—**Andrew Shaffer**, *New York Times* bestselling author

"This book made me laugh plenty, but it also made me think, something I usually try to avoid. Bachman's hysterical take on approaching middle age will resonate with every mama in the carpool line, but it's her ability to weave profundity into the mix that sets her apart.
—**Celia Rivenbark**, *New York Times* bestselling author of *You Don't Sweat Much for a Fat Girl*

"Kara Bachman has fast become the woman I want living next door to me. With her razor-blade wit and tell-it-like-it-is essays on navigating middle age (while tending children), she is exploring new turf, and the grass is super green and fertile. Readers will love her style, humor and stories that will make you guffaw and snort in public while reading. Middle age never felt so good."
—**Susan Reinhardt**, author of *Chimes from a Cracked Southern Belle* and *Not Tonight Honey, Wait 'til I'm a Size 6.*

"Just as I was sinking into the muck and mire of my own age-induced crisis, Kara's book rescued me with a laugh and a renewed hope that I'll never be too old to wear glitter or try something new. ***Kissing the Crisis*** is a hilarious and thought-provoking look at what all women face: the turning of the clock as we balance maintaining marriages, raising children and having careers, while trying to not to lose a sense of ourselves."
—Sarah Bonnette, Artscape columnist, *New Orleans Times-Picayune/* NOLA.com

KISSING THE CRISIS

Field Notes on Foul-Mouthed Babies, Disenchanted Women, and Careening into Middle Age

Kara Martinez Bachman

Fresno, California

Published by Quill Driver Books
An imprint of Linden Publishing
2006 South Mary Street, Fresno, California 93721
(559) 233-6633 / (800) 345-4447
QuillDriverBooks.com

Quill Driver Books and Colophon are trademarks of
Linden Publishing, Inc.

ISBN 978-1-61035-290-1

135798642

cover photo copyright CREATISTA
(Shutterstock Image ID:108138347)

Printed in the United States of America
on acid-free paper.

Library of Congress Cataloging-in-Publication Data on file.

Contents

Foreword

Not so long ago, in the early hours of a Saturday morning, I sat perched in a folding chair, binoculars pressed to my face, my hand on a notebook in my lap, and a half dozen people all around me doing exactly the same thing. Dawn was just yellowing the edges of the sprawling golf course on the other side of the suburban backyard.

Around the yard were a few small cages, outfitted with tiny trap doors triggered by a remote control. The woman on my left held it, the one with the killer trigger finger.

We were hunting hummingbirds. Well, hunting may be a strong word, and the passionate bird taggers around me certainly wouldn't have used it. I was just a spectator in this affair: the fall hummingbird migration tagging expedition.

Now, before that morning, trapping hummingbirds was a concept I found almost absurdly amusing, like Mr. Miyagi catching flies with chopsticks in *The Karate Kid*. These birds, after all, are tiny, Technicolor avian Speed Racers. How, exactly, do you catch that?

But this was a well-oiled operation. Trained folks gently captured birds and recorded their weights, getting a sense of the size and health of the migrating flock before releasing them back into the wild, where no doubt the birds thought: "What in the world was in that seed I just ate?"

As someone who wouldn't know a Rufous from a buff belly, clearly I was way out of my league. Luckily, I had a field guide to help me along.

I'm a big fan of field guides, those tidy manuals that lead us into unknown experiences with confidence. And that's what Kara Bachman has written in this hilarious new book about the most scary adventure of all: straddling that imaginary, hard-to-spot, but you'll-know-it-when-you've-crossed-it line from youth to middle age.

Crossing this line can be at times dreadfully boring and at others, giant-leap-off-the-high-dive scary. You close your eyes and hope you're making the right adult decisions for your family, your career, your spouse, when all you really want to do is plan your outfit for the next Duran Duran reunion tour.

Bachman writes with a sharp eye and a sharper sense of humor, celebrating life's absurdity and not giving in to the preconceived parameters of growing older. As she writes, rubbing Bengay on arthritic joins is oh-so-much cooler if you mix in some glitter.

As with any field guide, there's some lingo to learn; what exactly is a ukulele-harp Goth band? But once you've mastered it, you're in for a grand adventure. And Bachman is the best kind of tour guide: the one who really tells it like it is.

Susan Langenhennig
Home and Garden Editor, *New Orleans Times-Picayune*/NOLA.com

Introduction:
The Intoxicating Scent of Bengay

Carpe diem quam minimum credula postero.

Seize the day, trusting as little as possible in the future.

—Horace

SECTION I: WHY YOU NEED THESE ESSAYS

You may think that you are ready and able. You may look down at your quasi-comfortable shoes and up at your predictable and faintly lady-mustached reflection in the mirror and think you are equipped; I worry you are not.

On this, the dicey frontier called middle age, we women are easily lost and confused. Some of us cower. Some of us give it all a sloppy, drunken French kiss. Others of us, the punch-drunk, don't really know what the hell to do. This collection of essays was written to help clear the confusion.

Unlike most field guides by John James Audubon and whoever the hell else, there are no pictures. There aren't even hastily sketched drawings to accompany these chapters, each of which will relay a different question from this flaky new middle-aged landscape. There are no labeled diagrams of the things you'll encounter, no color graphics of the old women in stripper heels, or of the unlikely and ill-conceived dances with men who used to be German colonels, or of fights over rutabagas, or of the night I turned down Brad Pitt, or of southern drag queens who inspire. My drawing is always subpar, and at the time I was too busy (either observing or heading for the hills) to collect my wits or my sketch pad. Your imagination will have to color between the sometimes-caricatured lines.

Here's the thing. However deficient these essays may be, you can't set out there without at least the bare minimum of proper gear. You can't leave the base camp of spent youth with a sketchy plan, no coordinates, and nothing but a single bottle of Merlot and half a roll of chalky Tums. You need a trusty guide to identify booby-trapped pitfalls and possible opportunities for elation. You need a better pair of shoes. You need a special type of medicine, which I will cover in just one moment.

SECTION II: MEET YOUR GUIDE

I had always thought that "maturity" would be a slow process, with a kind of ebb and flow to it. I expected a slow drift current followed by a slight backwash—an undulating creep of realization that the youthful half of life was winding down and the adult half taking over.

It wasn't like that at all.

I had always absorbed the Madison Avenue image of middle-aged and elderly people, and I believed that a sure sign of throwing in the towel on youth was a focus on the mid-morning constitutional and the Fox 8 weather report using the Super Mega Doppler 5000. I also thought that the middle-aged must all feel pale and defeated, and that this was probably because they sometimes smelled like Bengay pain-relieving cream. All I saw were the beginnings of wrinkles.

Then one day, I realized I had the power to set out on my own unique midlife course. I remember the day. It was a far cry from what happened to Lewis and Clark, clad in their weird hats and suede moccasins, or North Face and Timberland jackets, or whatever on earth they wore. But I remember it all, the first sprints into uncharted waters that some unimaginative and judgmental fools may like to call a midlife crisis.

It just happened one day, this sort of psychological wanderlust. It may seem shortsighted to blame my daughter, Elaina, who was then a five-year-old with a frizzy mop of hair and endless enthusiasm. In fairness, it wasn't her fault I grew bored with domestic routines; it was not her fault I longed to escape by back-bending dizzily into my own childhood, into old hobbies and my old love of licorice, and into sticker collections and first dates and lying in the sun; it was not her fault I wanted to revive the times when everything—the good, the ugly, the bad—still lay ahead, untainted. It was not her fault her mom wanted to put on an old T-shirt and some jeans and take a spin around a roller-skating rink. It was not her fault I wanted to do all this to the musical accompaniment of something awful and dated, such as Air Supply.

But if I were in the mood for the blame game at this moment, I'd have to say it was her fault entirely. She unwittingly did something that made me careen off the deep end of the linty navel-gazing pool—she started kindergarten.

That darn kid.

When her older brother, Dane, had started school a few years earlier, it had been like a refreshing eucalyptus shower. The days with only one child underfoot were suddenly free of the complications and competitions of sibling rivalry, free of endless comparing of the grilled cheese sandwiches to see whose was better melted. But when this last baby walked away from me one morning and into the world of phonics and homework and cafeterias, everything changed. She didn't know that when she walked out to that school bus, holding hands with her brother, she immediately took my thoughts away from washing pajamas, planning meals, and taking temperatures and turned them over to grislier, more important philosophical ponderings, such as "What do I do with my life now?" or "Of what use am I to anyone now?" And of course, let's not forget the always important "What the hell is there funny to look at on YouTube today?"

We all know, with the exception of the YouTube ponderings, that much of this is pointless foolishness. *Of course* I was important and, frankly, necessary to my kids and husband. *Of course* my parenting when the kids came home every day was valuable; it would surely determine whether or not my son would get in a good college, or whether my daughter would end up as a teacher, a doctor, or as some girl dancing with flimsy mandated-by-law pasties.

They needed me. For the mac and cheese. For the permission slips. For cuts and scratches, bloody and raw. But suddenly, what I was doing no longer *felt* important. Suddenly, without a kid pawing at the hem of my skirt (er . . . sweatpants . . . who am I kidding?), without a constant reminder, it felt so . . . lame. There was no stay-at-home-mom razzle-dazzle. There was zero glory.

There are only so many times a person can clean the ungrateful toilet or empty the wastebaskets. There are only so many times a person can read the mail. These workaday clock-watching hours were like forced rides on roads to nowhere, where hot blacktops narrowed into unclear horizons and sent up boozy-looking fumes.

So, as soon as the realization hit of what was going on in my own mind—namely, what was being born was some kind of so-called midlife crisis—I came up with a detailed plan to deal with it all. It is based on sound scientific knowledge of medicine, on a complex understanding of healthy human psychological behavior, and on the glam rock movement of the late 1970s. Let me run it by you, just to see if it passes muster.

Section III: Essential Gear

Here's the surprising two-item checklist of what you'll need:

1. Some tubes of Bengay.

2. Glitter.

Go ahead and use Bengay, but make sure to put on tons of glitter at the same time.

One requirement of this plan is that they must always be worn together. Colored glitter, applied over the pain-relieving cream. (It is unfortunate this combo product is not on the shelves already. Get with the program, marketers!)

Longevity scientists, psychiatrists, and, no doubt, middle-aged Mary Kay Representatives have discovered there is a certain texture to a large dollop of Bengay, slathered just right, that makes it the perfect foundation for a bit of gleam. But when you use it, follow these directions carefully, especially when out in the field without a tube of cherry-colored lipstick or a poly/cotton shirt bearing a somewhat sexy animal print.

When you put the cream on, make it beautiful. Fan out the dollop from the edges of your knees, starting over those sorta achy kneecaps and trail it on up your thighs like a wild kudzu vine. Go ahead and cover a few of those varicose and stretch mark trails while you are at it (doing that won't hurt a thing). Make it look like a big glittery tattoo, a rebellious badge of being a certain age in-between. Make it a beauty mark, like a shiny port-wine stain. Revel in its smell.

Sometimes you can even dab it on the crook of your elbows, for no particular reason, when you are feeling just fine. Put it on the upper chest, which always hurts from raking leaves. Go ahead and place it in its own leafy pattern there. When you sprinkle the glitter on top, try to use an iridescent white. It will appear as icicles, as some kind of early fall frost.

One caveat: it will seem at first smelly and antiseptic to your husband and your coworkers and your dining partners and your kids. They will think you are sucking on a whole bunch of cough drops, or have just been to a very glamorous and sort of pervy doctor. But just do it: be not afraid.

This plan may sound ridiculous to some youngsters who have never walked the bunion-and-spider-vein wilds, but I support it wholeheartedly. It is sound.

In addition to this body glitter tool, I have had many promising break-throughs about how to deal with bearing the tribulations and trials of middle age. As your guide, I have all sorts of theories and outlines and step-by-step plans, none of them having anything to do with either prunes or Engelbert Humperdinck. I know you may, at a few points of your journey through these essays, question my credentials or question my wisdom. I will forgive you if you ever have a thought such as "Who are you to talk? You're still just perimenopausal." It is quite possible you have already been there and done that, have walked the menopausal woods and glens and prairies in Bengay and stilettos and made it out alive. You may be older than I, and may think that at only age forty-five, mine is a *youthful* midlife crisis. But I say it is never, ever too soon to indulge in a good thing.

It may appear now that by telling you this—about how I feel a little bit young yet a little bit worn out—and stuff about Bengay and body glitter— that I'm trying to give you some kind of metaphor for your life. It may seem like some kind of recipe for those deep questions about midlife that we will all face. It may sound as if I am comparing the glitter to an atti-tude of acceptance you should adopt, applied liberally across the parts of your life that seem just "old" enough to give you pause. It may sound as if I am saying to "make the best of it" when you stare in the mirror and see ever-deepening age lines and ever-larger pores and those god-awful little spidery red veins. If it makes you feel better to think I have something touching and lofty to say, go right on ahead and believe it.

But honestly, I'm simply saying—*especially* when you need effective gleam for some roller skating—if you wear Bengay, stick some sparkle on it . . . *quick.*

1

How I Turned Down Brad Pitt

"Remember that the most beautiful things in the world are the most useless; peacocks and lilies, for instance."
—John Ruskin

Once, about twenty years ago, I turned down a night with Brad Pitt.

How, you may ask, does that happen?

It all unfurled just before I was married, before he became a producer, aged backward as Benjamin Button, or showed us his butt in *Troy*. Before a word like "Brangelina" made any sense.

Although my memory is foggy on the exact words, it went something like this:

My Roommate: "Wanna go bowling? We're going with Brad Pitt and you're invited."

Me: "What are you talking about?"

My Roommate: "Brad Pitt. The guy from *Thelma and Louise*. Know that book *Interview with the Vampire*? Well, they're making a movie out of it and he's here in New Orleans for filming. My sister met him."

Me: "You're serious?"

My Roommate: "Dead serious. They met at a club last night. He wants her to bring a few friends. I'm going, and she thought he'd like you, too. We're meeting tonight at Rock'n'Bowl."

Me: "I can't bowl!"

My Roommate: "Don't worry, he'll like you. And best thing is if you run out of stuff to say, you can just stand there and look at him. I'm sure he's used to it."

Why, why on God's green earth, you may ask, would one of *People* magazine's "Sexiest Men Alive" want to go bowling?

If you ask that question, you've never been to Rock'n'Bowl. Also known as Mid-City Lanes, it's one of those places that are one-in-a-million. In 2005, Hurricane Katrina forced it to relocate. But back in the early '90s, back when I said no to Brad Pitt, it was still in the same space it had inhabited for decades.

It was probably built in the early 1940s, during times when pins were still set by hand. The invention of the automated pinsetter popularized the game until the golden age of this "sport" arrived in the '50s and '60s. These were the years of people wearing shirts that had "Walter" or "Lenny" embroidered on the chest and "Andy's Radiator Repair" screen printed on the back.

By the early '90s, Rock'n'Bowl had borne the scars of all these years. Its neon sign still shone and stuttered, lighting the route for drunken leaguers to find their cars after a tournament or night out with the guys. The floors had scuffs and scars from hundreds, or thousands, of balls being thrown at them.

You could almost *feel* the history in there. You could feel the hook-ups made, where first dates surveyed their girls from behind when they were up for ball. You could feel hearts broken to sounds of pins falling, and you could sense the mixed feelings of those who hated bowling and were dragged along with a crowd. You could feel the good-old-days of slicked-back hair, pedal pushers, and bouffants. You could sense the bell-bottoms, feathered bangs, and Bay City Rollers. You could feel the mullets and Rubik's Cubes and safety pins through noses. You could envision teens of grunge, roughed-up jean bottoms scraping wood lanes. You could see the modern kids, pant waists inching toward knees.

This neighborhood jewel featured live music, mostly by Cajun and Zydeco bands. I would wager to say that Rock'n'Bowl is the only place on the planet where one can yell out "Strike!" to accompaniment of live washboards and accordions. Some local band or other would joyously set up shop among the pitchers of draft and nachos and pins. They'd usually wail down on their instruments in ways that are a little gritty. They never minded the pins clinking on wood, a kind of percussion.

There's usually dancing taking place as well, happening at the blond wood lanes. I have seen people two-stepping with ten-pound balls in their hands. They'd really get down, even while wearing the ugliest damn shoes in the universe.

The sexiest man alive obviously wanted to check out the place with his sky-blue eyes. Perhaps he wanted to hear music. Perhaps he wanted to "hang out." Maybe he wanted to wear a bowling shirt that said "Brad" just above his washboard abs and directly on top of his chiseled pectorals. He wanted to wear those ugly shoes. He wanted to meet . . . me.

And what does a woman of age, as I am now, twenty years on, do if in such a position? Does she run in for a bit of quick Botox? Get a pedicure, making sure to choose a color called Cherry Madness? Would she spend hours trying on the coolest designer Manolo Blahnik bowling shoes (surely this product must exist, for exactly these moments)?

Here is one thing a middle-aged woman in the midst of a midlife crisis would *not* do: she would not say no.

She would not say no to going bowling with this man, under any circumstances. If her child were graduating from high school, she would hand her husband a video camera and say, "Tell her I wish I could be there. Get me some video of it. I'll be back by midnight."

If her dear beloved dog of ten years has just passed away, she'd say, "Put that thing on ice until tomorrow. I have some pins to take down!"

If she had a crick in her neck from holding the phone at work all day, she'd solve that problem by cutting off her neck. But she *would not* say no to meeting Brad Pitt.

But since I was only twenty-three and didn't have the wisdom of age, I said no.

I had just met my husband-to-be, Tim. I loved him, and still do, as much as it's possible to love a person who hadn't come out of my own womb. I loved him more than Italian sausage pizza, more than crème brûlée. I had more feelings for him than Brad Pitt had muscle packed into his derriere, which is saying a lot.

But these thoughts still ran through my mind:

"What if I'm hanging around with all these A-list celebrities and lose my anonymity? Could I still go to Walmart undetected by paparazzi?"

"What if Brad decides I'm the perfect leading lady to star in his next film, and I need to move to LA, half a continent away from Tim?"

Of course there was the best of all, the question still conjured up purposefully at times when I need a laugh:

"What if Brad falls for me, and I have to choose between Tim and Brad?"

These are the thoughts of someone who is twenty-three. At twenty-three, we're romantics. We still believe the endings of movies. We have big, watery eyes. If you could somehow draw a picture of our souls, the portrait would have eyes like characters in Japanese anime—huge, reflective, dual abysses that reach deep inside but see only possibilities and never ghosts. Back then, there was one thing we definitely would have all believed in: the notion that a sexiest man alive could somehow cause us a dilemma.

A married forty-five-year-old woman does not have such thoughts. Here is what she thinks:

"I'll go bowling so I can have a good story to tell next time the ladies and I have coffee."

Or,

"He's rich. Maybe he can pay for my bowling."

Or, more than likely,

"Damn, it will piss Tim off if I go bowling with the sexiest man alive. I'M THERE!"

And that's the extent of it. We of middle age *have* been around the block a few times. We know the evening would likely end with the sexiest man alive acting perfectly nice, then bugging out after a quick game and humble nod. We know nothing unusual would happen. We know the bowling, even at Rock'n'Bowl, would be so ordinary that we'd need creative elaboration when telling our tale for the next coffee clatch. We know we'd need a big fish story and hope it flies.

You see, even though she might still run off for the last-minute Botox, the middle-aged woman has seen enough to know that talk of French fries and bowling form would be the likely conversations. Why? Because despite what you may think, this is what people talk about when bowling, even people with rock-hard abdomens.

Gals who have crossed the zenith of that "over-the-hill" hill accept that our bowling companion may be A-list, but we already have the *real* sexiest men alive.

The really sexy ones are waiting for us at home. They're the ones sitting on our couches, grinning like boys because they secretly took the remote control when we got up to pee. They're the ones cutting the grass, sweaty bellies sticking out from under yellowed T-shirts. They sweat for us to have something green. They're the ones waking at first light, becoming yes-men against their better instincts. On good days, they feel fine because their sports team has won, or a meeting went well. On these days they will not only show us their love, but they'll even talk about it, too, and act like we're beautiful.

The *real* sexiest men alive are snoring in front of the TV while we bowl, because they're tired from working to pay for the dream house and college fund. Their feet are up, propped on top of our stack of women's magazines featuring photos of a certain Mr. Pitt. They're tired from loving us so hard.

Unlike the young, most forty-and-fifty-somethings have had, at some point, men at home who see *us* as the sexiest women alive. They love to look at us despite the saddlebags and gray hairs we keep having to pluck. They stand by us. They do not duck out after a quick game. They stick around, always letting us choose which restaurant we'll go to, which video we'll watch. They rarely comment on our form. They build something with us every day, something worthwhile and, in some instances, everlasting. And we know that nobody in a bowling shirt saying "Brad" could ever have an effect on any of that.

So we middle-aged ladies, we're unafraid. We go bowling. We stare at the abs, unashamed, with absolute glee.

2

A Midlife Renaissance

"Middle age is when you've met so many people that every new person you meet reminds you of someone else."
—Ogden Nash

I knew I was on shaky new terrain when I finally met up with the Dark Ages. I walked among decked-out, frilly, Tudor-inspired college kids, old hippies seeking an even older truth, and gossamer-winged faeries with lower back tats of scrollwork and gangrenous-looking emerald-tint Celtic knots. I met these people at a Renaissance Faire.

If you don't know what a Renaissance Faire or Festival is, don't fret; let me paint a portrait. These are festivals that attempt to re-create pre-sixteenth-century Europe. They offer period entertainment, food, and demonstrations of medieval and Renaissance-life. There are usually carnies high on mushrooms selling leather goods and retro Dungeons & Dragons–inspired art and overpriced patchouli incense. There are funnel cakes.

Almost all participants are members of a club called the Society for Creative Anachronism (SCA). The SCA is a nonprofit, tax-exempt educational organization that primarily concerns itself with portraying the "truths" of medieval life.

Based on what one witnesses at a Renaissance Faire, the observant will go away having learned important lessons, such as:

- Medieval people seemed to have a penchant for crafting garments of synthetic polyester. (Is this the aforementioned anachronism?)
- Back then, there was an abundance of pub wenches wearing Wonderbras and punk rock dirndls to be found in the general medieval and Renaissance populations.

- Approximately 80 percent of the people of Europe were noblemen or royalty.

- There was quite a bit of pot smoking that went down in the Middle Ages.

Once all of the important educational stuff like this is covered, participants will concern themselves with displays of combat using plastic kiddy swords and shields made of PVC and duct tape (ancient crumbly documents written with quill pens prove the historical accuracy of such materials in armor construction). They will face off against each other in the ring, clad in full armor. Some will wear gear that must be frowned upon by the purists—protection pieced together from some old soccer shin guards and modified football uniform padding. Some of them, the ones who have the money for it, will cover themselves with reproductions of the garb of actual knights: worn and battle-ravaged leather gauntlets; decorative bowl helmets and headpieces with jingly chainmaille attachments hanging behind the neck; heavy molded breastplates that make themselves momentarily appear to have fine pectoral muscles instead of manbreasts. They will also walk around eating turkey legs with their hands and fail to use any kind of hand sanitizer prior to this feat, so as to seem authentic to the core.

It must be admitted that I sometimes enjoy the sound of plastic clinking against plastic in the heat of a realistic battle. There is something about seeing men dressed as if they gave a crap that is exciting, and is probably what roped me in. Granted, there are a few unruly college kids in the plain white tunics that must have been the era's version of the tagless Fruit of the Loom that modern guys seem to think looks good as outerwear. For the most part, however, there is a lot of color, many ruffled piratesque shirts, and hints of the "slash and cut" styling that was popular in Renaissance-era fashion. The best part: occasionally, a very enterprising or slightly effeminate guy, usually a theater student, will go whole hog and dress a little like Shakespeare.

So, I look into the idea of our family joining the ranks of these indigenous, Fruit of the Loom tunic-wearing peoples. I do some online research, make some phone calls. What could be better for our family? What could be more humorous? What is better than learning and playing dress-up at the same time? And what better way to associate with peoples who are primitive yet still too evolved to waste their precious time at silly Star Trek conventions?

I'd never been a joiner of anything and was nervous about all this. We had always, out of a sense of, well, lethargy, avoided joining things. I did not have a single membership aside from a grocery discount club—and outside of the beer aisle, the events surrounding that rarely involved high, imaginatively dressed posers. So, here is how the conversation with my kids went:

Me: "Kids, you remember that Renaissance Festival we went to a few months ago?"

Elaina: "Yeah, that was fun."

Me: "How would you like to start going to lots of things with those cool people, a kind of remembering-the-good-old-times club? It will be fun, there will always be funny costumes to laugh at."

Elaina: "I'd love to be a fairy princess there!"

Dane: "Can I kill people with swords?"

Me: "No, but you can pretend."

Dane: "Well, I guess that's better than Boy Scouts, you're not supposed to pretend kill people there, probably."

The first "meeting" I attended for this organization was held on a week-night evening in the fall, at the home of a couple who had been involved with the SCA for many years. Their home exterior, to all outward appearances, was a normal abode—white siding, quaint weather-worn porch, big shed. The lawn was nicely manicured, and the common but beautiful crepe myrtles were still lingering in awkward bloom. It was dark outside, and a single bulb from the shed cast a skinny sliver of light across the lawn.

There were several guys milling around in the yard, comparing weapons, seeing who was alpha male, seeing whose PVC rod was more badass. They seemed to approach each other not with a jovial spirit that would be expected, but with the competitive edge of athletes; they meant business.

A sporting pair, two teenage boys, wrestled on the lawn, shouting as they kept count of something that appeared to be game points.

One guy, a lanky older gentleman wearing miniscule reading glasses, was visible through the open door of the shed. He seemed like a serious craftsman, busying himself with inspecting the quality of what appeared to be pieces of quaint armor, long poles, foam padding, and rolls of duct tape. It was an unusual assortment of apparatus, none of which were commonly found in the average athletics store.

There was a central figure milling about among the men, a dude named Sir Lawrence. Sir Lawrence seemed to be about five feet five inches in height. He was clad head to toe in fighting armor. He wore the typical aluminum breastplate affixed to his front smock style, with leather straps on the sides. He wore a heavy-looking helmet that had a rectangle of metal extending down over the face, protecting the bridge of the nose. Roman style, there was a plume of some kind of hair jutting out of the helmet top that resembled a red horse tail. The pants were not so much pants as they were knee breeches, leather trousers tied above the knees. He also wore a pair of Adidas tennis shoes.

When he removed the horse tail hat, I could see he was of ordinary looks; he wasn't handsome but wasn't exactly ugly, either. He appeared to be in his mid-forties and was one of those rare specimens that seemed the same thin weight he had been as a teenager, which was fortunate given his small stature. His hair, trailing down his back, was captured in a loose ponytail and seemed to be part landed gentry, part David Lee Roth.

What was notable about this guy, aside from the small fact that he stood on a lawn in the Deep South in 2009 dressed as a cross between a medieval knight and a Roman centurion, was not immediately clear—but there was something. The other men seemed to show him a particular deference, as if he were their superior. They agreed with his every assessment; their eyes darted to him often for guidance and comfort. It wasn't until I was introduced that all the pieces fell into place.

"Kara, meet Sir Lawrence. In the 'mundane world' he goes by the name of Chris," said the man with the mini-spectacles, who had left his post in the shed and begun the introductions.

"Nice to meet you," I said, a little unsure of myself, a little unaccustomed to the processes and customs and etiquette of "joining stuff," particularly this kind of stuff.

"Welcome!" says this Chris of the mundane world. "And now for an authoritative introduction to the ways of the SCA. I am equipped to guide you since I've been involved for the better part of thirty years, from the time I was a wee one. And now I have reached the level of knight, and you must know that few achieve the level I have attained."

He said all of this with an unusual cadence, and with an ever-so-slight feigned British accent. His tone reminded me of those period dramas that we chance upon late at night on public broadcasting channels and watch reluctantly when there is absolutely nothing else on.

"Oooh," I say playfully, thinking I am funny. "A knight! Are you going to fight for my honor? Offer me a rose? Should I give you my scarf to hold? Do you know Merlin, by any chance? Are you a member of the Round Table? And, is the table really round, or is that just a myth?"

And he stares at me. He stares at me long and hard, without so much as the crack of a grin, or the upward wiggle of a lip. He is stony.

Now, I am immediately concerned for the future of this conversation. How does one go on from there? Do I bow? Apologize? Do I beg him for a crust of dry, wholesome, brown bread?

"What I mean to say is," I start, in an act of contrition. "You are a knight. That's cool. This must be fun for you to have stayed involved for so long."

"Fun?" asks Chris, glaring at me with a look of incredulity. "Are you kidding? This is not fun. This is a passion. This is an endeavor. It is not fun; it is difficult to aim for perfection." He flicks his pony-tailed hair back over his shoulder. It was held in its neat bundle by a hair scrunchie, which was probably lifted from his wife's junk drawer in the upstairs bathroom.

So I give the only response to this Mundane Chris that I was able to muster:

"Um, okay."

Now, roundabout this time I have an inkling that there are some interesting things about this Society for Creative Anachronism, one of them being that apparently some of its members are not doing this because they think it is fun, but because they may actually believe they are part of a mission—a crusade, of sorts.

In the course of the night's conversation, I would come to discover from other members that Mundane Chris had no discernible means of making a living and that he was, at the time, a "house husband." Not that there's anything wrong with that. I have heard of house husbands. In fact, I know a few. The problem was not with the husband part of that equation, but with the house part.

As we all know, looks can be deceiving. We know, when we ride the streets of suburbia, that behind the facades of the homes we pass there may be a fleck of dirt on the floor, or a shirt or two unwashed, or even a large pile of *National Geographic*s from the years 1954–1997 in the middle of the living room floor. We know this. We accept that in the United States of

America a man's home is his castle, and he is free to keep it as he sees fit. There is an unspoken agreement that as long as he keeps the grass mowed and takes down the Christmas lights before February, we do not care about the fact that the drapery does not match the upholstery inside, or even that the upholstery is covered in those godforsaken clear plastic protectors.

But holy hell! Nobody in this great nation of ours had anything like this particular house in mind when they agreed to the inspired notion that every man's home is his castle. And there are few in my position who would have not turned around and high-tailed it out of the "joining something" mode the moment they saw what I saw.

But you must know that by now there was no way I could turn and walk away. Women in the middle of a midlife crisis do not do such things. They do not turn in the face of danger, or while at the cusp of disillusion. I can recall at that moment knowing that life almost required me to stick around there, whatever the cost or result. These are the ways of women in my current position: there is no backing down. Seriously, when would I ever have the chance to witness this again, when I only had about forty or fifty more years to live, and those years were just ticking away?

And here is what I saw:

A living room, faux painted to resemble a medieval pub. There were dark smudges that were crafted with care to resemble dirt (had someone with the plague inadvertently rubbed a carbuncle against the drywall?). There was some type of large ceiling beams installed, painted to appear rough-hewn and crafted with primitive tools.

There was a full wooden bar, creaky and held together with rusty iron nails. This bar was lined with antique glass liquor decanters, each filled with a different earth-toned concoction. I became convinced that someone had deliberately applied dust and grime to these booze decanters, for it was fairly perfect as far as medieval grime goes. I will go to my grave believing that those people had fake dust in their home. Can you imagine it?

Dane: "Mom, you know you're old now, your mind plays tricks on you, and your memory gets foggy. There is no such thing as fake dust!"

Me: "Don't you tell me I'm losing my mind! I know what fake dust looks like when I see it!"

So, here I am, looking at the fake dust, wondering why I am always adding glitter to things while these people add synthetic dander to their glassware. And then it hit me, squarely: maybe their dust is my glitter. This is what makes them feel alive!

11

Here are the other things that make them feel alive: the head of a dead boar, taxidermied, with the body of a fake raven clenched in its underbite. Call me crazy, but in my home we enjoy a candlestick or two, a vase here and there, but have never considered a boar eating a raven to be something that gives off a vibe of feng shui.

Other items of curiosity included a framed and matted picture that I recall from a PBS documentary as being that of Vlad Dracula; various furniture that appeared handcrafted and upholstered of animal skins; and a curious item that seemed to be a . . . gulp . . . laptop. There was a shelf that ran the entire circumference of the room, at about five feet off the ground. Its sole purpose was to display the hundreds of beer steins, primitive mugs, and wood and horn drinking vessels that Sir Lawrence had apparently acquired on trips to foreign lands (oh, you know the lands, places like Houston and Mobile). Some of these seemed to be not only souvenirs, but also prize cups bestowed upon Sir Lawrence for various acts of showmanship, bravery, or skill with weaponry. Some were engraved.

And here is the best part of what was in that room: a coven of witches. Yes, I am pretty sure that there was a coven of witches in the room, looking up at me as I walked in. There were about ten of them. One witch, quite literally, as you would read in a fairy tale, had one creamy eye. That bum eye looked like blindness but also spoke of some kind of mystical insight. None of these women wore makeup; none wore clothing that seemed manufactured past 1932. There were no brassieres on any of them, and believe me, there should have been. There was an eerie silence among them as they busied with the work of women: they looked through McCall's and Butterick pattern books; they did a little Middle Ages–themed embroidery through antique wooden hoops; or, they just sat there, surveying me with suspicion. They all wore babushkas over their hair, and someone, during whispered conversation, said the word "pagan."

Not that there's anything wrong with being a pagan or anything. It's not my place to judge. As a lapsed Catholic, my own religion today amounts to simple admiration for whatever unidentifiable spark lies behind, above, below, and in nature, and which does stuff both sorrowful and zany, such as making hurricanes and mountains and fake medieval dust. But I suspected these women were pagans of another order. I suspect they were casting spells without the use of glitter.

I swear I am not making any of this up. I also do not make up that this home had an entire floor, the whole upstairs, devoted entirely to sewing the fine raiments for this organization. The witches took me up there as part of a very unusual grand tour. The tour began in the communal, open-to-the-public kitchen obviously shared every evening by errant knights, ladies-in-waiting, merchant-class profiteers who were presently collecting unemployment, and a single blacksmith who probably worked on weekends at a video rental store. I was escorted up the stairs, past several darkly lit bedrooms that seemed draped in velveteen fabric, past eight or ten suspicious cats that meandered on the landing or in the laundry room doorway, and into the massive sewing room, where there was a wide table for cutting patterns and measuring lengths of fabric, modern white sewing machines lined up in rows, and the parts and pieces of half-completed muslin tunics, tapestry robes, Elizabethan collars, and God knows what else.

This night was the beginning and end of our association with the SCA. I decided that making stews with feverfew and horehound and hyssop in a communal kitchen in the Deep South was just not my cuppa tea. And besides, high-waisted gowns with synthetic piping and boob compressing bodices do not flatter my body type even a little bit.

My husband and I still take the kids to the Renaissance Festivals, where they can slay invisible dragons and eat turkey legs with dirty fingers and watch the jousters in mock battle with long balsa-wood lances. But this experience did something to me. It killed any interest I had in joining anything, particularly the SCA. I guess that part of the middle-life panic is now satisfied—and it only took one night.

Oh, by the way, did I mention that in addition to all the other decor, Sir Lawrence's wedding photo was on the wall in his living room? It was held in a heavy gilded frame, matted with reverence. He appeared in full armor, and his new bride posed as a queen with a jewel-studded medieval crown. They stood arm in arm, stiffly perched in front of the iconic Cinderella Castle at Walt Disney World. And can you believe that in this picture, they were not laughing, at all? I think if they had been laughing, or even smirking just a bit, or even had the faint, ironic trace of a grin, I may today be in the SCA. But alas. 'Tis not to be!

I left this all behind me that night when I walked out and away across that wooden porch worn down by the boots of Crusaders and the leather sandals of serfs. I clomped out quickly over the floorboards where no doubt performers had sat a few times at parties, high as kites and playing wooden flutes and dulcimers and handcrafted drums.

I have looked back, however, and wondered why I didn't ask that cream-eyed witch to give me some decent lottery numbers. But I try not to focus on regrets, so will consider this no further.

3

Ukulele-Harp Gothic Pop/Rock Trio

"It takes a long time to become young."
—Pablo Picasso

I need to keep my fingernails cut short nowadays.

That is probably a good thing, as it will prevent the taking up of nail bedazzling as part of this recent midlife glamour-spreading regimen.

There have no doubt always been big nails around throughout the annals of time; no doubt even the women of early civilizations donned such symbols of sexual aggression that bespoke a tiny bit of danger. There have always been such weapons.

There were nails aplenty among the inner-city girls of my youth, festooned in an array of colors and exotic detailing: glued on plastic slivers highlighting the digits in lime green or fuchsia; the dangerous-looking, clawlike growths of a predator, bestudded with iridescent rainbows or holographic stars; or, for the more tasteful nail fetishists, a smooth and nude "French Manicure" that looked almost like the slick hood of a car, or the naturally shellacked underside of a cowrie shell.

I had never been a fan of the use of nails as either weapons or show-pieces. It seemed a time-consuming and vain endeavor that always ended in heartbreak when a nail broke. Also, the question has never been sufficiently answered as to how one attends to certain personal functions with three-inch nails, each one shellacked with the image of a four-leaf clover. How do you adequately pick your nose? Insert a tampon? Chop down a tree? Weld the bow of an aircraft carrier? I have also wondered—most perplexing of all—when a woman has little rhinestones glued onto her claws, how, exactly, does she make meatloaf?

It is clear that for some women, there may be useful purposes to such overgrowth and adornment. It is understandable that some may feel the glamorous look attained while hitchhiking or shooting the middle finger at fellow drivers outweighs any meatloaf encumbrances, especially when in the midst of a midlife crisis. But for me, it simply does not work. Form should follow function.

In recent years, I have instead been a proponent of the following "look": nails a little brittle and yellowish, cuticles red from chewing, clipper cut straight across to the nub. I have been trying to bring back a look, unconsciously or not, which surely was quite popular during the Great Depression, as well as during the Summer of Love.

I wear my nails in this fashion primarily because I play the harp. Now, surely many people out there are wondering, "The what?" But you know full well what I am talking about. You know I am talking about the instrument you hear when someone in a romantic Lifetime Movie Network production is going back in time and remembering. We all know the characteristic "going back in time" sound of a harpist's digits rapidly rubbing across a few octaves of strings to craft steadily raising and lowering glissandos. As far as most people know, that is about all a harp does. It stands in an orchestra just waiting, waiting for the "going back in time" moments like this one:

[Young couple stands hand in hand in a field of wildflowers. Random butterflies alight.]

Fabio Romeo: "I love you so much; I cannot imagine what I did without you by my side. I cannot imagine what it was like before I had you to hold, to make me feel whole again."

Feminine Woman: "My heart goes out to you and always will. It will be only you, for the rest of my life. I will always remember the day that we met, the day you saved my life!"

[Harp glissando plays. Special effects make image on screen appear to fog up and wiggle around ("going-back-in-time wiggle"). We have now gone back in time. Feminine Woman hitchhikes, one purple rhinestone bedazzled thumb held in an upright position. A Rolls-Royce slams on the breaks, and the man, very buff, with an angular jawbone and smoldering eyes, drives up alongside Feminine Woman and her large nail.]

Fabio Romeo: "I almost missed you, but then I saw the glint of the afternoon sun on your best hitchhiking nail and knew it was meant to be."

Aside from setting such beautiful scenes, the harp is widely recognized as an accessory carried by the cherubs you see on Valentine's Day cards. Apparently it is used by these chubby and precious ones to create some ambient music as Cupid goes around and shoots arrows into people, which usually has the express purpose of making them lust after Jake Gyllenhaal.

To play the harp, a cherub floating in the heavens (or a woman sitting on her suburban couch) needs to have short nails. It is impossible to pluck the strings with even so much as a millimeter of nail extending beyond the nail bed. Were you to try playing without clipping first, you would end up with a mixed-up jumble of sounds, with random clanging thuds and muddled, buzzy plucks that sound more like a cell phone vibrating on a table than like any type of angel's song. Since I am in the novice years of learning my instrument, a set of Lee Press-On Nails would be an especially bad idea, despite their indisputable sophistication. A few would be lost with each arpeggio.

Except for the fact that we all have short nails, there is little else in common between the average harpist and me. I am not slim. I do not have long, flowing hair. I do not own cats. I will never have some dumb "Bless This Home" Celtic cross-stitch hanging over my front door. I have an inflexible policy that I will only play "Greensleeves" during Christmas week. I also have the very specific goal of never, ever learning to play "Danny Boy."

Here's the thing about the harp. Most people do not realize that the harp is also a required instrument in the most unique of musical genres popularly known as Ukulele-Harp Gothic Pop/Rock. If you do not know about this genre, which has grown from there being no bands of this type last decade to there being one band of this type this decade, then you are very much out of the loop. And it can be said definitively that our household has been solely responsible for this surge of popularity.

What, you may ask, is a Ukulele-Harp Gothic Pop/Rock Trio, and what do they play? More importantly, why do they bother to play it? The following *Behind the Music*–style true-life scene will give you a glimpse into how such a creative force in the music industry had its beginnings:

"Hey, Tim," I say to my husband, "quit playing 'Stairway to Heaven' on your uke. I am practicing my 'going-back-in-time' glissandos and can't hear myself! You are too loud!"

"To hell with 'going back in time,'" he says. "You need to do something different, something a little Gothic yet somehow still cutting edge, like 'losing of the mind and going crazy.' Don't you get sick of always conforming?" And I see that he has a point.

"Well," I say, "I wonder what would happen if I tried out a little of that 'losing of the mind and going crazy' with your 'Stairway to Heaven.' I could toss in some chords now and again, too, and make some wails that sound a little like Robert Plant!"

And with this, something new was born.

Why this collaboration was born and why it persists is a mystery. No doubt, as this type of music is in its infancy, it will be some time before it begins to take off and have mass appeal. The Top 40 charts still have seen nary a ripple from this growing musical movement—but we are working on it.

Some time ago, Tim and I held very limited auditions for a lead singer. We sought someone with charisma, with drive, with a real edge that screamed Uke/Harp/Goth/Pop/Rock. We chose my then six-year-old daughter.

Elaina: "Hey, what is a stairway to heaven? Can we get one? And what is a bustle in a hedgerow? What is a hedgerow?"

Tim: "Just sing and leave the analysis to the musicians."

Since that time, we have really honed our craft. We have moved on and increased our repertoire to include some of the great works of the 1980s, namely the music of Tears for Fears and Weird Al Yankovic. Things are taking shape.

Sometimes when performing for packed audiences sitting on our living room couch, I remember my first band, Perpetual Motion. The year was 1983. I was the keyboardist, and my eighth-grade friends, Marny and Vicky, made up the rest of the trio. We spent hours choosing that name. Perpetual Motion. It was genius! We spent many afternoons discussing the aesthetics of our girl band modeled on Duran Duran. We wrote stuff in notebooks, always spiral bound and usually covered in stickers showing David Bowie dolled up as Ziggy Stardust, or rainbows, or the intentionally cryptic first letter of someone's name (usually that boy in math class).

Here is what we decided: our clothing and haircuts would always be styled asymmetrically. We would try to look like women in Patrick Nagel paintings at all times. We would pout our lips. We agreed that we could use Sun-In bleach on our bangs, but that any wholesale hair color changes had to be approved by "the band" beforehand. We would look modern and have a sound that nobody could deny was anything other than "girl group Duran Duran." We would be in perpetual motion.

We never played a gig. We never learned the instruments. We never bought the instruments. But we did once walk into a music store in the mall and oogle that one teenage sales boy with nice cheekbones. He had smiled at us. He had known from our slanted and dyed hair what we were there for. He took a break from selling clarinet reeds and boring spit valves and trombone cases to show us the cool New Wave sounds that a Roland synth could make.

Many years had gone by since the Perpetual Motion days, and the dream had fizzled. There had been no motion, no forward trajectory at all, no stone rolling toward the limelight. Not a note had sounded. We just got more zits. We just grew up.

But roundabout the time you reach the point of having to slather on moisturizer instead of benzoyl peroxide, something happens deep in the soul. Something happens that suddenly brings back yearnings for perpetual motion. The year that we started our trio was when I crossed that moisturizer Rubicon.

For many years, I had not even considered something as wild and ambitious as joining a ukulele-harp gothic pop/rock trio. The demands of parenting and paying the bills and keeping some rambunctious kid or other from spilling Kool-Aid on said bills had occupied too much of my time. I was too tired for Perpetual Motion. I was too tired for Slight Motion. I was just tired.

But when your last kid goes off to school, and you are free to explore, and to play, and to make that stupid song that had lain dead silent for two decades, you set your sights again on getting that first gig, on taking pouty band photos, on recording that first demo that nobody will ever hear. Never mind that in the photos with you will be a cheap 26-string harp and a middle-aged man with a uke and a receding hairline. Never mind that you are fat. Never mind that you start every song over four or five times before you can get it right. Never mind that the members of the band play in different keys. Never mind the dramatic falsetto of the six-year-old. At least you are in a nerdy and tentative jerk forward. You are on the move.

It was decided that if I were ever going to make it big in a uke-harp trio, it had to happen soon. So I finally grabbed up some gumption and clung tooth and nail to those infinitely wise words of Horace: "*Carpe diem!* Seize the day!"

4

Big Ass Beers and Sports Freaks

"Men do not quit playing because they grow old; they grow old because they quit playing."
—Oliver Wendell Holmes

Occasionally, forty- and fifty-year-old women just need to let crazy-lady loose.

You would think that it would all be out of the system by the time middle age hits. During the precious and exciting years of young adulthood, most of us cover lots of territory: stints of all-night bar hopping, in dark fraternity-themed taverns that will play, at least five times a night, the songs "Brown Eyed Girl" and "Sweet Home Alabama"; dinner parties paid for with exhausted credit cards, where we first learn to mix a reasonable drink and the men pretend to actually enjoy smoking cigars; frenetic nights on the dance floor, spent sweating and swaying to the music, jerking our inebriated selves back and forth like human metronomes. You would think our need to "live it up" would be exhausted by the time we reach age forty or so.

But no. This is especially true when a long hiatus, aka that huge blank space on our dance cards known as childrearing, separates us even from the memory of such things. After countless nights of diaper changes and endless days filled with phonics drills and temper tantrums and cookie batter smears on the upholstery, going out on the town feels, somehow, completely new.

In fact, the further I get from my young adult days, the more pressure there is on any given night to pull myself off the couch, put on a bra, smear some glitter over the excessive body hair I failed to wax, and simply boogie on down.

Despite the desire, however, I rarely do this. Most other women in my position do not, either. They want to, but they don't. Why? Is it because it is more fun to stay home and fight with their husbands over the remote control? Or, is it because we think it is (somehow) more meaningful to stay up late practicing the times tables with our fourth-grade children than to stand around laughing and drinking a cosmopolitan? Is it because we know that if we were to do an all-nighter, or even a part-nighter, we would still need to get up early in the morning? Is it because we fret that our kids would open their eyes the next day at the crack of dawn, wipe the sleep away from their jolly little faces, and jump on us in bed just as the hangover is kicking in? Or, is it because we know that when we just stay home, our raggedy old too-tight short shorts with the missing waist button would not cause anyone to look the other way?

But every once in a while, when the planets are aligned just so, we manage to find a way to paint the town red, regardless the obstacles. We find creative ways to let loose, whether we have children or not. We find the particular restaurant, the particular bar, the dance club or the movie theater or the park bench that makes us feel like teenagers again. We long to recall those feelings, long lost in the responsibilities of raising a family.

Also, sometimes a woman in the midst of a psychological crisis just wants to hang around with a bunch of drag queens.

There . . . I said it.

Sometimes I want to be inspired by those who have more facial hair than I do but somehow make it appear that they have less. Sometimes I want to absorb an attitude that there can never be too much of a good thing, and that DayGlo-colored mascara is completely appropriate, even before Labor Day. I want to surround myself with the colorful boas and random sparkle that is left behind on the pavement, and the real inspiration that comes from such entertaining but outcast miracle workers, honest-to-goodness magicians who mold their own selves into whatever they fancy. Sometimes I want to mold myself as well, out of sweatpants and peanut butter and jelly sandwiches and into a middle-aged southern Marilyn Monroe, too chubby and with bad skin, yes, but with wind blowing up my dress and with panties slightly visible that do not even resemble mom-drawers.

A lot of enjoyment can be had when you are out and about around drag queens. There is never a dull moment. There will never be a discussion on potty training, or a detailed description of what everyone ate yesterday at

Applebee's. You will never have to hear boring corporate stories, tales of monogrammed golf balls getting stuck in a sand trap, or bitching about how their mutual funds are performing. But you will hear a lot of *this*: "You go, girl!" Which is *exactly* what I am interested in hearing.

Since coming over the crest of the hill (you know the one—the "over-the-hill" hill), I feel a particular kinship with such masters of disguise. My makeup is starting, at times, to resemble theirs. I used to never wear lipstick, settling instead for a quick slathering of lip balm between diaper changes and baby feedings and trips to and from the school. The hair was rarely styled and was instead worn short so it would air-dry without assistance. I let the zits show, for all to see.

But now that I have more time, and more worry, the new older face staring back in the mirror waiting for its paint requires a few more gallons, a base of primer, and multitudinous trim and edging tools. On special occasions, it is painfully elaborate. I have returned in recent years to sometimes looking in the mirror, returned to smoothing, vainly and *in* vain, the frizz on top of my head with "products" that are quite different from those used the last time I cared for such things (mousse, anyone?). I have taken to using lipstick and now have an affinity for heavy foundation. My eyebrows, crooked and splotchy from twenty years of angry plucking, now require some careful drawing on. I *need* to draw them on, and thick! The bigger the brows are, the smaller the apparently growing schnozz appears to be. It's an illusion. None of it is working, but I'm not ready to give up or give in just yet.

And here is another tool of illusion, the one that I cling to like a life preserver, the one that I hope against all odds will make me seem less tired: eyeliner. Sometimes I wish someone would invent an eyeliner that could make forty-and-fifty-somethings appear to be less tired of *life*—now *that* would be a little pencil of magic that would actually be worth shelling out a few bucks on.

It is unpleasant, feeling the need to doll up like this. It is new for me, a person who never catered at all to things about appearance. I can even remember thinking as a child:

"All the old ladies who wear eyeliner must be hookers!"

The current trend of things shows that I will probably end up being an old hooker, according to my own rules. If this pace of facial decoration continues, I'll end up as a big-nosed, eyelinered, suburban granny whore.

Do not be surprised if I end up with my own street corner, my own sexy granny routine. You'll see on that corner displays of the newest "Hootchie Granny" fashions: bedazzled orthopedic stripper shoes with peekaboo toe cutouts, perfect for the foot fetishists; comfortable cotton underwear, thong style, each decorated with graphics of a different position from the Kama Sutra; and an appropriately sexy bustier, with Velcro easy-open closures that are gentle on the arthritis. I'll do a cabaret dance around a chair, or around my walker. I will paint the tennis balls stuck to the bottom of the walker legs in an erotic shade of cherry red.

Until then, I intend to fit in a few final premenopausal prances around town. My husband can come along . . . he's no bother at all.

A few years back, I got the hankering for such a prance. Unable to find a babysitter for our kids, my husband and I did the only thing that really makes sense: we brought them along to watch us get drunk. They joined us for an afternoon of wandering this nation's skankiest thoroughfare, Bourbon Street.

Since I am a native of New Orleans, our family often visits the French Quarter. Although most locals deride it as mainly for tourists, for me it is like a big, smelly, colorful scrapbook of memories. We love to visit many spots in this antiqued and beautiful city that all certainly have something to do, at least in a roundabout way, with getting laid.

Although this aspect, this getting-laid business, played little part in our agenda, it seemed to be the purpose of most people there. If you have never been to the French Quarter, you have missed out on a real experience for the senses. You have missed out on the wrought-iron balconies of some of the oldest homes in America, standing side by side with crumbling and beautiful French Creole cottages. You have missed the cluttered streets and the sidewalk next to where the old Opera House once stood, with its low curbs so that horse carriages could easily pull up onto the pavement and escort hoop-skirted ladies to the door. You have missed some of the best old restaurants in the world.

More important, you have also missed the drunk college tourists eyeing every female they pass; the prostitutes peddling their wares; the genteel and polite older couples, walking hand in hand in lightweight seersucker; the tacky T-shirt shops, selling taxidermied alligator heads and tasteless Aunt Jemima statues; fat old men with their attractive trophy women in high heels; local street kids and their mangy dogs, waiting for you to drop a coin in a top hat to pay for the next piercing or dye job; the hipsters and club kids doused in the ecstasy of MDMA, en route to the nightclubs you say you would not get caught dead in but slyly survey from the corner of your eye when passing by; the kooky neighborhood characters; the artful and creative locals, too involved to know that their weird conversations frighten the tourists; people singing the blues; people dancing with joy; people picking your pockets; and best of all, women in midlife crisis.

For some, the best time to be in the French Quarter is during the Mardi Gras season, the several-weeks-long bacchanalia of parades, balls, and parties, during which everything just described still exists, only in Technicolor.

We chose this particular weekend for our visit to this favorite neighborhood because it was Labor Day weekend, during which is held the Southern Decadence Festival, which is often described as akin to a "Gay Mardi Gras." And no, I am not making that up; there were actually those who felt the regular ole Mardi Gras was not gay enough.

As a drag queen aficionado, could I let Decadence weekend pass without making at least some kind of showing downtown, without some sort of visit, however brief? Could I pass on the chance for even one gander at something more festive, and significantly more fun, that what we find on our normal weekend strolls through the mall? Could I miss out on seeing the impressive costumes, the fine tailoring, and the expertly applied eyelashes? No, I could not.

So, we are there in the Quarter, my husband and I with our two (then elementary-aged) children. Although we mostly restrict ourselves to the tourist areas where people are usually sure to have on clothing, the kids make a sideways glance down the wrong street and get their own accidental gander at something that, to them, is just a little bit unusual.

"Why is that man's butt mostly showing?" says my then innocent daughter, Elaina, pointing at the offending party. And there is a man, a very buff and "decadent" man, wearing nothing but a dazzling, sparkled, and feathered G-string jock strap. He also wears some kind of militaristic shoulder pads that appear to be those of a soldier, and a huge sequined helmet you would see on a very glittery and steroid-pumped Achilles strutting around in while on his day off.

Now, under most circumstances, when a six-year-old child says something like that, something having to do with men and butts, it is quite expected that you will have a moment of shock followed closely by an abundance of concern. But seeing as we were downtown during Decadence weekend I was not surprised, and remain to this day impressed with how I held myself together. I looked into her eyes with the certainty of an expert and said the only rational thing a mother could say:

"He lost his pants," I said in earnest, "and he had to dress as a gladiator wearing teeny-tiny underwear because the only store open today to buy new clothes was a costume shop. That was the very last costume they had, and it was a few sizes too small."

And her answer, because this explanation made perfect six-year-old sense:

"Oh, okay!"

After this exchange I laugh to myself a little, and begin to feel comforted when I realize that other mothers from time immemorial have probably said the same thing to their probing daughters when presented with similar circumstances. The gladiator costume, teeny undies. It has probably been used as many times as the story of the baby-bearing stork has been told.

After this touching mother-daughter moment, I felt an urge to hug her but could not because I had a Big Ass Beer in my hand.

A hug is pretty difficult to execute when holding a Big Ass Beer. It is purchased in a plastic 32-ounce tumbler from the Big Ass Beer place on Bourbon. The plastic cup, in an act of marketing genius, reads "BIG ASS BEER" in a clear font and a typeface that is very large but not quite big ass. This beer is too large for a woman to hold with only one dainty hand, so I needed to use both. And let me tell you, it's hard to give your daughter a bear hug over talks of teeny gladiator costumes while holding one of those suckers.

So, we are walking along, sometimes shielding our kids' eyes from, and sometimes drawing their focus to, things that are fantastic. There is great diversity here on this strip of bars and restaurants and shops: great smells of crawfish and cocktails that waft out into the streets; great things to touch in the "authentic" voodoo souvenir shops, filled with the icons of Catholicism and Africa; great funk and Cajun music that is the end all and be all after a 32-ouncer. We reach a point in these intoxicating wanderings when my mostly quiet son Dane stops walking and says, enigmatically:

"Am I going to burn in hell with the sports freaks?"

And I say:

25

"Huh?"

And he says:

"Look at the sign. They list all of the stuff that will make you burn in hell, and our family seems to be quite a few of those things!"

Although at this point the Big Ass Beer is mostly empty, I still have enough focus to read the sign he referenced. It said:

You will burn in hell if you are a:

Jesus Mocker

Murderer

Atheist

Pornographer

Gambler

Drinker

Homo

Sports Freak

Thief

Fornicator

Shopaholic

There may have been a few more vices listed, but I cannot now remember them all. The guy holding this large sign was middle aged, like what I had just become. He wore very respectable glasses, a large wooden cross around the neck, and a baseball cap that said "Walk In His Footsteps." He was not at all decadent. He looked pained, and was crying out in desperation to the transvestites and tourists and damnable kids and drunken moms in midlife crisis for some kind of repentance.

Now, I do not want to be accused here of being a *Jesus Mocker* or anything of that sort. And one must concede that a woman walking on Bourbon with a very large and watery-tasting American beer in a tumbler may not be setting a good example for her children. But I take exception to this guy's list of offenses.

I will gladly tip my hat to the inclusion of murderers and thieves. But in all honesty, didn't he think it was taking things a tad far to damn someone to hell for enjoying big-box retailers too much, for going to the mall every year on Black Friday, or for loving back-to-school sales? Did he think it was a stain upon the soul to watch too much sports, to fancy an afternoon of the Vikings vs. the 49ers? Is he somehow convinced that God does not want us to paint our faces in team colors? And what, pray tell, are we to make of tailgating? Does heavy tailgating, with hot wings and all, require a confession? And even more disturbing: would the required act of contrition be having to sell those great season tickets on the fifty-yard line that took so long to get? Of course, the next logical question stands to reason—what kind of dastardly image are we inadvertently giving to barbeque?

I myself see no particular virtue in afternoons laced with chips and salsa, pigs-in-a-blanket, halftime discussions, and play-by-play accounts of large dudes moving around on fake grass carrying a ball. Perhaps it would interest me more if the *cheerleaders* were actually dudes, fabulous queens in team-color pumps, randomly tossing glitter on the Astroturf and saying: "You go, girl!" But then, that would probably double, or even triple, the supposed sinfulness of football, so America will surely have none of it. And we can be pretty damned sure the NFL would not be too keen.

If I see that non-decadent forty-ish guy the next time we are on an afternoon stroll through town, I will be sure to offer the following advice: Reshape yourself. Just do it, no holds barred. Use DayGlo mascara. Use tolerance . . . use empathy . . . or a spicy hot wing rub. Use *something*.

But at the very least, I'd say to him, reshape your sign. Go ahead and keep *Thief* and *Murderer* on your list of offenses, but please scratch out *Sports Freak*. Replace that one with something that makes more sense. My much-analyzed and wholly generous vote goes to: *Old Eyelinered Hooker*.

5

Gunshoot Jamboree

"From the middle of life onward, only he remains vitally alive who is ready to die with life."
—Carl Gustav Jung

I had never shot a gun in my life. As a child, my parents never owned guns. My father didn't hunt; he had always preferred the slightly less bloody sports of hiking and gardening. I had reached adulthood without being exposed to guns in any way, shape, or form.

As a child I had many conversations with my mother about guns, and she expressed a real distaste for those who toted. She passed rigid judgment upon people who enjoyed the destruction of mammals that had large, flirty lashes and the eyes of a doe (makes sense that these mammals had doe eyes, since they were often, in fact, does). She didn't think there was anything wrong with eating meat, of course, but *did* think there was something a wee bit sinister about people who wanted to kill and prepare their own. As we lived in one of the more violent metropolises in the country, she had heard her share of the stories of devastation that occurred at the point of a pistol. Basically, she hated guns and distrusted people who used them. These opinions were passed on to me without question.

She would turn over in her grave now to know that in the past few years, I get a real thrill out of shooting stuff.

You can calm down now if you are concerned. I have never shot a doe as it lazily grazed by a riverbed or as it jumped over brambles as if they were hurdles at a track meet. I have not shot at squirrels or even at mischievous rats. But I have shot at cans, buckets, padded walls, bull'seyes, and paper targets that resemble Osama bin Laden. I was probably only able to do this because Osama did not have long flirty eyelashes.

And you may wonder—how does a dainty lady of five feet two, with six-inch wrists and hands so small they are both needed to hold a 32-ounce beer, become a gunslinger? Well, if you had ever been invited to a Gunshoot Jamboree, then surely you would not need to ask this question.

Although I have been to only one Gunshoot Jamboree, I assume the protocols are generally the same across the board for this type of function. One would guess there are no fancy silver-embossed invitations containing RSVP cards and flowery language. One would guess that there are no chocolate fountains or doormen or pieces of melon wrapped in prosciutto at the other Gunshoot Jamborees that are held throughout the year in this great nation. In my estimate, most of these soirees are, instead, of an impromptu nature, and are spurred on and inspired by some variation of a singularly important ingredient that can be found in many cellars and basements across America: a jug of homemade blackberry wine.

Now, don't you get to thinking all snob-like, feeling somehow superior to me as you read this. Please recall that sometimes when traveling, it is required to "do as the natives do." I've heard that when traveling to China and dining in a private home, it is considered the height of rudeness not to finish every bite on the plate. I do not know if this little factoid is true (may have gotten China confused with Kansas or some such place), but if it is, you can see how leaving that fried crab Rangoon thing on the plate might be a wee bit rude.

So this is the position I found myself in on that day: drink these fermented blackberries, or risk looking like a bad guest. So I drank it. And damn! That stuff was the best root cellar–based wine I had ever had! There must have been strict temperature controls to produce such a lovely bottle. Great pains must have been taken to ferment it in that old five-gallon water cooler bottle and consciously place it far away from all those onion bulbs, the ones that were dug out to overwinter in style. Or, could it be that we had sampled a particularly good vintage, a year that saw optimal rains and perfect sunshine?

Since we were in the Ohio River Valley of Southern Indiana, it is doubtful the reason for such a fine-tasting beverage had anything at all to do with optimal weather conditions. The Ohio Valley gets its share of rain. And when it is not raining, the sky is trying hard to look like it wants to. In the valley, there is a constant depressing haze that lingers over the horizon, casting a blanket of gray for months of the year. It is a blanket that seems to cover almost everything, seems to almost cover *you*.

The reason we were there in Indiana is that we were visiting my husband's relatives—Belinda, her husband, Tommy, and their teenage son, Ryan. We didn't visit often, as the twelve-hour drive was unpleasant with two kids in the backseat fighting over which DVD to play and debating about who was stupider and uglier. Belinda and Tommy live on a large plot of land, so fields, trees, and lots of cute mammals trying to avoid becoming a meal surround their home.

The acreage surrounding their homestead was almost idyllic in its charm. There were large fields of rolling hills visible from the patio behind the house, and each was backed by an undulating line of trees that touched the horizon. They were in fall display. To the left there were a few acres of crops growing, the anxious product of a modern-day sharecropper's labor. Nearer in, there were sheds and outbuildings to store the farm implements. There was a crumbling old treehouse in an oak near where we sat, no doubt the place where Ryan played when he was younger and imagined himself in the Swiss Family Robinson. There was a swing made of a single plank of wood attached to a rope, suspended from a tree branch too high to imagine. This was, no doubt, the best tree swing in the world.

We were lucky on this particular day, because Tommy's parents joined us. The cool thing about this couple is that they somehow lent an instant ambience to this jamboree, much in the way that a paper palm tree or hula dancer decoration lends a theme to a luau. I love those kinds of people, who are almost a walking theme; they are stereotypes of such proportion that they instantly become almost as a decorative cardboard cutout, propped on the table, next to the cake. Tommy's father was such a character, a kindly man who seemed almost as if he were in costume.

He wore faded blue jean overalls. These were not the overalls that you would see on a teenager, or on a pregnant woman (why do pregnant women always feel the need to wear overalls?). These were work clothes, stained with earth, faded from many washings, carrying the scent of an oil rag. He wore a straw hat, a millenary creation of the Huck Finn genre. It had begun to fray on the edge of the brim, right in the places where he always grabbed it to remove and replace. You will rarely meet a man that seems more placid than this one, or one that seemed more like Winnie-the-Pooh.

His wife was a lovely woman, the kind of grandmother we all want. She was all about having fun; she was the kind of person who didn't need to put glitter on stuff at all, because it already shined. It appeared that she went about all things with gusto. She enjoyed long rides on her motorcycle, and wore the clothing of someone much younger than her seventy-something years. She was sharp, and witty, and caring. This was an Auntie Mame of the countryside, feasting incessantly on life. She decided to take off her clothes and jump into the nearby above-ground swimming pool, for no good reason at all. It was freezing cold. Ryan, with his youthful zest, changed into his swimsuit and followed.

As you can see, things were already a little unusual, what with Winnie-the-Pooh sitting there chewing on a piece of straw (cue the country folk!) and granny jumping in her bra and panties into a four-foot aboveground.

Well, one wonders, what exactly does one do when a jamboree gets to this point, the point where old women begin to disrobe? My husband had the perfect answer, the only rational solution: you play the harmonica.

As a child he had learned to play. When young he loved this instrument, one that could go anywhere hiding in his pocket, one that served as a friend and confidant. When he spoke to it, blew his words and feeling through its core, the harmonica somehow understood, somehow translated.

After years of disuse, his old harmonica weirdly and coincidentally ended up in our car for the long drive north, no doubt as part of the contents of the plastic toy bag filled with Barbies and Matchbox cars and rubber lizards. And then it somehow ended up in Dane's pocket as he sat there fidgeting in that molded plastic chair on the patio. And then it ended up, after so many years, rubbing against my husband's lips.

My husband was rusty and out of practice, but somehow able to recall the sizzling-hot Top 40 harmonica tunes we all know and love, tunes such as "You Are My Sunshine" and "This Land Is Your Land." He was able to expertly suck and blow through those little metal squares and make it sound like the most celebratory of music. There was much dancing of the country kind. There was actual knee-slapping, which is something I'd never witnessed in person in my life. Belinda continued to pour the wine.

After a bit, we became hungry from all of the fancy dance steps. The Pooh decided it was time to feast.

Zen Master Pooh: "Need to get us some roastin' ears."

Me: "Some what?"

Zen Master Pooh: "Some roastin' ears. Don't need to make it fancy, you can roast by microwave, just wrap it in one of them there paper towels and it'll come out just right."

So I am thinking: what kind of ear is this? *Is this a doe's ear?*

Me: "But what exactly is a 'roasting ear'?" (And yes, I did try to focus on saying the "-ing" at the end of this word.)

Zen Master Pooh: "Never had a roastin' ear? I'll show ya."

He walks down to the nearest field, a huge patch of green with seven- or eight-foot-tall plants. I am worried for the does, hiding among the greenery. I also wonder, just a little, if he will come back with a big jug of honey, sealed with an old cork, and followed by a trail of bees.

But no. He comes back with an armful of corn.

Me: "Oh, *corn*! Ears of *corn*!" I say, relieved.

Zen Master Pooh: "Yeah, I knew you've had that before. You just microwave it and add some butter, and you got something really good."

You will want to know details of Pooh eating his roastin' ear. I can tell you that it was funny. He looked like a human typewriter, taking precise little bites, one row at a time. The corn moved back and forth at his lips, and he started a new row when he got to the other end of the ear, as if someone had just hit the return key. Rest assured that you have never seen anyone eat corn in exactly this way. It looked like a corn harmonica; was this turning into a full-on jam session?

Surely, roundabout this time you are thinking: "How much more quaintness can I stand? How much simple folk living, how many plainfolk anecdotes could be told that have not yet been?" Well, unless you have been invited to one of these jamborees, you don't know that the most critical element has not yet taken place in this story. Unless you have been to a jamboree, you don't know that for it to be complete, there needs to be some shooting at stuff.

That apparently is a favorite pastime of Tommy's. At about six foot four, he is a very imposing man, especially when he is holding three or four guns at once. Like his mother he is a biker, a lover of the open road, a fanatic for hairpin turns and hills and truck stops with diners. He has turned many bikes onto their sides on rock-littered asphalt roads. You can bet those roads are always curvy. God only knows how, but he has had all-terrain vehicles roll on his back with nobody at the wheel. He has had scuffles. He usually sports the requisite look of black jeans, black boots, wallet chain, and a bandana-like wrapping around the head. He is intimidating.

Now I know you would like to hear that when the guns and the holsters and the chunky brass rounds came out onto the patio, that I stood up for what I believed in, that I gave some speech of this order:

"We do not *want* our kids exposed to *guns*, so would you *mind* putting those away until the kids are inside? We see guns as a symbol of *violence*, and don't want our innocent children believing that playing with guns, hunting, or any kind of violence is somehow *cool*. We find all of this *distasteful* and would prefer if we now all go back to the slapping of knees."

But I didn't say this. The actual conversation went more like this:

Tommy: "You ever shot a gun?"

Me: "No."

Tommy: "Well git your ass over here and shoot this fucking thing."

Me: "Okay."

And little did he know the can of worms that he'd opened.

He gently pressed the grip in my hands and transferred the loaded gun. It was heavy. The grip was warm. Tommy watched me and took a few slow drags on his cigarette, blowing smoke up into the dismal sky. I tried to steady my shaking hands and aim at the soda can perched in the distance.

I shot the fucking thing.

There was something about the power of firing it, the power of having death extending from the tips of one of my fingers, which felt *great*. I did not mind the shock to my frame, the huge kickback that made my hands hum and burn for more than three minutes afterward. I did not mind the ear-shattering *pop!* of a firing gun that I had finally heard for the first time in real life. It cannot be helped but to think that Tommy forced this gun in my hand at the exact right time, at about the time I turned forty. Maybe somewhere in the back of my mind, in this shattering and destructive frenzy, I thought I could shoot down what was happening. Maybe I thought I could take haphazardly aimed pot shots at the old hourglass before it could empty of any more sand. Before I could get . . . older. Or, maybe I just liked destroying stuff, which, looking back, is more likely the answer.

I can remember wishing we had shot more more on that autumn day. It was disappointing when we had finished testing out the .38 and when our experimenting with the rifle was done. The other firearms were too dangerous, too old, too precious, or too fiercely stunning for me to mess with. Tim and Tommy had at those, however, with reverence.

In the end, we had destroyed quite a few beer cans as Tommy showed us every weapon in his arsenal: "This one is an old Russian gun . . . that is Soviet shit right there," "This one is a Nazi Ruger, someone may have shot an American with this sucker," and so on. Apparently there was some history connected with these killing implements. Impressive.

And so the Gunshoot Jamboree comes to an end. The wafting scent of gunpowder slowly dissipates from the patio as we polish off another bottle of the wine and wait for the sunset. We spend the last minutes of twilight looking through high-powered binoculars, surveying the white bouncing tufts of deer tails, creatures oblivious to the fact that they had just escaped, by a mere half hour or forty minutes, a drunk and frenzied firing squad.

This jamboree was a first for our family, and we loved the novelty of it all. The roastin' ears were delicious; the company was genial; the harmonica hummed.

I also somehow came to understand Tommy's obsession with guns. I understood that the same drive for excitement that made this hobby his passion would later fuel my new interest in shooting at Osama bin Laden posters at the neighborhood range. Maybe sometimes he just needed to hear that *pop!* sound out dangerously over the din of the nine-to-five and bill paying and TV watching. Maybe he felt that sometimes being alive needed to entail occasional moments of power, and of risk, and of momentary deafness. When you are around forty, you don't get much of that, unless you suddenly decide to buy a Chuck E. Cheese's franchise or become an astronaut. Although we cannot ever blow holes into that rapidly emptying hourglass, we can imagine, for a few moments when we are shooting at stuff, having power over things that seems unstoppable. We can imagine doing serious damage to something, even if that something is nothing but a thin piece of paper with an ugly Taliban bull'seye.

6

Wonder Bread for a Frenchman

"In the multitude of middle-aged men who go about their vocations in a daily course determined for them much in the same way as the tie of their cravats, there is always a good number who once meant to shape their own deeds and alter the world a little."
—George Eliot

One way many people deal with an identity crisis in midlife is by channeling the need for status and validation into works of charity.

They are evident everywhere, the kind men and women who submit to all manner of volunteerism. In fact, it is almost a cliché that as one eases into middle age and later, there is often a need to "give back" to the world. Such participatory members of society gleefully populate the Parent-Teacher Associations. They run for office and coordinate sales of chocolate bars that hopefully will fund gym suits and chalk. They infiltrate the United Way and the local dog shelters and the Red Cross. They knit caps for babies and make nubby, metrosexual crochet sweaters to be worn by hulkish men stationed overseas. They also make quilts and host plate luncheons serving low-cal macaroni salads. They give. They wear name tag stickers on their shirt pockets, self-consciously printed—in easily readable letters and brand-new Sharpie ink—with their husbands' surnames. Mrs. Johnson. Mrs. Fallow. Mrs. Schexnaydre.

And dammit, you better listen to them. You better listen and do it their way, or everything will get all messed up. The fundraisers will fail, homeless dogs will roam the streets, and, even worse, the Fall Festival paper plates will not match the napkins!

This is not to imply that everyone who takes pride in civic involvement is a control freak or power seeker. Some of them want to end world poverty. Some of them care about things like clean water, and about fostering empathy, and, pragmatically, about having enough glue sticks to last at least until the firstborn buds of spring. I am just saying that some of them are control freaks and power seekers, and we know damn well exactly who they are.

They are usually the ones carrying clipboards.

The clipboard holders are the ones with loud voices. They also, in the very worst of cases, smile that smile where only the mouth is involved, but not the eyes.

You may find me volunteering for some small thing or another. You may find me speaking out against evil. I may buy a silly rubber bracelet in some show of solidarity. I may wear some kind of ribbon-shaped pin, or leave a few coins in a jar. But you will never find me carrying a clipboard. Ever. Even more sadly, I do not care if the plates do not match the napkins. I do not care if the awards ceremony after-party serves subpar generic brand tortilla chips instead of Doritos.

This is not to imply that I do not respect this very responsible desire to change one's life by changing the lives of others. This hackneyed notion of "getting through giving" can actually have some merit. I understand that when some women look back on their lives and decide it is time to do something with it, they see "involvement" as somehow more meaningful than indulging in looking at old pictures of David Cassidy. But how, oh how, could they come to such a conclusion? How?

General fits of volunteerism hold little interest for me; I have never wanted to assume leadership of anything at all. I also have never been the overly generous type—self-sufficiency has always seemed the way to go. I have always admired the values upheld in, for instance, Laura Ingalls Wilder's Little House series, where self-sufficiency is paramount, and community is a give-and-take that should serve all parties. The complete altruism of the preacher has always bothered me almost as much as the selfishness of Nellie Olesen has.

However, I am not altogether without moments of generosity and good-will. For instance, many years ago while in college, I spent some time traveling in the South of France with my predominantly-straight-acting-gay-repub-lican-freethinking-capitalist-conservative-yet-slightly-hedonistic-best-friend, Randy (don't even ask. Just see if you can figure that one out on your own). We were scheduled to spend the night at the home of a couple who lived in the sleepy southern town of Montpellier. We made this last-minute arrangement for lodging in the traditional way, as it has occurred, perhaps, from the beginning of time: we were visiting "friends of a friend."

In the name of common courtesy, and to show gratitude for their kindness, we decided we needed to show up at our hosts' door in the apartment block with some kind of offering. What could we bring? A nice bottle of wine, perhaps? Nah, too much of a cliché (and what did we know about French wine, anyway?). Some flowers? No, too expensive. How about . . . some baked goods?

We worked our way through the winding cobblestone streets, following our noses past old homes and sidewalk café and window boxes filled with perfectly fake-looking real petunias. There were people strolling the streets. There were middle-aged ladies in flat shoes hurrying home on bicycles, carrying brown paper sacks with stuff like a few lone tulips sticking out of the top. There were dogs on leashes, following their owners into places that sell cheeses and smokes and bottles of Fanta. Eventually, we caught the waft of yeast in the air, a purely delicious smell that indicated a bakery was nearby. When you are in France and catch that scent, you know you are in for a treat.

The bakery was filled with every imaginable type of sweet and savory confection. There were éclairs lined up in a row, each with a dull coating of chocolate frosting that seemed irresistible. There were mouth-wateringly light croissants. There were beautiful honey-colored blocks of pain au chocolat, airy bread infused with chunks of cocoa-based deliciousness. Every puffed-up, chocolaty, fruit-topped, hand-whipped confection of your dreams was there.

And what did we buy? Why, of course the only thing that made sense: a long, hard piece of bread.

This was one of the last days of our trip. The till had run dry; only a few lone francs rattled around in our unlaundered pockets. We purchased what we could with the change: one plain baguette, approximately 30 inches in length. French bread, a single stick. Delicious, but as a gift, it was on par with bringing a loaf of Wonder Bread to someone who lives in Dallas.

And here is where my huge show of generosity comes in:

Randy: "I'm hungry. Since getting off the train an hour ago we haven't stopped walking at all. This is enough. I'm gonna eat this baguette."

Me: "NO, you can't eat the baguette, it is a gift. This baguette is all we have."

Randy: "But I am hungry! I can cut it neatly in half and we can bring them the other half. It only needs to feed two people; there is enough that they can each have a piece."

Me: "We will not bring them half a baguette! We need to bring the whole thing! They might think that we are cheap and ungrateful! Who brings half a baguette as a thank-you gift? *We need to bring the whole thing!*"

So, clearly, I have had my generous moments.

I have even, over the years, had the thought cross my mind of starting my own charity. For instance, it would be nice to start a charity for people so poor and clueless that they would consider bringing half a stale baguette to a Frenchman as a thank-you gift. But in my maturity, I have come to this conclusion: some things are lost causes.

I also conclude that the rabid civic and charity involvement of middle-aged women wearing pastel-colored capri pants and golf shirts is not about the cause for which they fight, but is about beefing up the obituary. Yep, I did just say that: beefing up the obituary.

> *JANE DOE (1962–2010)*
>
> *Jane Doe has passed away from hypertension caused by the stress of organizing too many bake-a-thons. She had tirelessly devoted her life (or, at least, the second half of it) to volunteering for the North Side Elementary PTA, the Red Cross, the Concerned and Involved Women's League, and a local SPCA-sponsored supper club for fans of literary works inspired by the beauty of tabby cats. Everyone who knew her knows that she derived no personal gain from her community involvements, especially when the bastards she organized refused to do things her way.*
>
> *She will be laid to rest at the Shady Oaks Cemetery on Main Street. In lieu of flowers, donations may be made in her name to the Half a Baguette Foundation.*

Now, surely this type of cynicism may be rubbing some of you the wrong way. It should. I have mixed feelings about my stance on this issue. Sometimes it does seem a bit grinch-like to be so critical of people who have the gumption to do good. Any soul worth its salt must appreciate the generosity of people who are willing to donate, to stand in lines, to make phone calls, to knit, to collect, to serve, to listen, and to bend over in the sun. Sometimes I think it should not matter one whit why such civic involvement reigns supreme in the middle-aged and retired. There are moments of recognition where I see clearly that what matters is that some good does actually get done.

Rarely, at other times I may even seem to be, deep inside, a little like the civic-minded. Occasionally there are flickering moments of vain concern when considering what my own obituary would read if I were, perchance, to kick off anytime soon:

KARA MARTINEZ BACHMAN (1970–2016)

Kara Martinez Bachman has passed away from complications associated with the inhalation of too many hair dyes and glitter-based products.

She has tirelessly devoted her life to filling her children's lunchboxes with sandwiches made of stale bread and finding the energy to change their bed sheets once or twice a quarter. Everyone who knows her knows that she derived no personal gain from anything other than singing karaoke in a bad Pat Benatar impersonation.

She will be laid to rest amongst the people who have all volunteered, at least in the second half of their lives, for the local Red Cross. In lieu of flowers, donations may be made in her name to the Rock and Roll Hall of Fame in Cleveland, Ohio.

The risks of such obituaries aside, I am content sitting by the sidelines watching as the other mothers smother each other in the PTA frenzy. I watch as they volunteer and donate and run relays. I watch as they train for 5Ks. I watch as they falsely praise each other. I watch them in both amusement and awe. I recline back in some bleacher or another, pretending to read a high-minded magazine while I actually look sideways at their saccharine and judgmental gaggles. I spy on them during halftimes and intermissions and breaks in very important meetings, surveying their altruistic tableaus through cheap pink dollar-store shades specifically chosen to mask the suspicion, and the jealousy, and the wrath.

I wonder—do they all know they are just using this as an exercise to feel important? Do they know that it simply makes them feel vital, gives them a new purpose? Do they know that it takes away their middle-aged, or old-aged, restlessness? Do they know that it pretends to fill the slots left by their vacant husbands, or by their growing and passive kids who have recently forgone hugging them good night? Do they know that it is a stand-in for their lost dreams, which have shrunk into nothing more than angry fists in their hearts, closed up tight? Do they know that it is not really about the charity at all? Do they know that it does not make even a tiny bit of difference whether the theme for the prom is "Under the Sea" or "Over the Rainbow"?

About this time you are probably thinking it would be wise for me to just shush up about all of this. You are probably thinking that instead of showing my unattractive side, as I have here, I should instead try to emulate such women. You think I, too, should channel any regrets about the past and apprehension about the future into good works instead of into navel gazing. And you are probably right. But you are thinking this without knowing all of the facts, without knowing the project I work on secretly, behind the scenes.

You do not know about the foundation I have started, the one for jealous, lazy suburban women who listen to songs like "Imagine" through brand-new headsets while sitting alone in the bleachers: Midlife Rationalizers Anonymous.

7

The Bar and Grill Loophole

"The first half of life consists of the capacity to enjoy without the chance; the last half consists of the chance without the capacity."
—Mark Twain

Our educations partially happen in that unsuspecting place where we encounter the *real* ideas: a local bar. It's where the notions we might carry through the years—stubborn albatrosses—first took shape. Paradigms, both dumb and not-so-dumb, are born nightly, like drunken phoenixes rising from Marlboro smoke.

You know the conversations we had, because in all likelihood, you had them, too:

"Where does the universe end? And, if it ends, what's on the other side?" or *"If you were on a lifeboat and had to toss someone overboard to survive, how would you decide?"* or *"If God made everything, then who made God?"*

I always ended the night smelling like fermented hops and cigarettes. I didn't smoke and hated the smell of the things, the pungent stench of tobacco mixed with burnt embers. But in some strange way, the smoke that wafted deep into my hair and shirt fabric somehow reeked of the sweet smell of success:

Roommate: "Um . . . you stink, Kara."

Me: "Yeah, I had a great time. We thoroughly examined Aristotle's Primum Movens cosmological argument over some Guinness. And oh, yeah, I learned to do the Moonwalk."

More than twenty years ago now, in 1994, Tim and I planned our honeymoon—a monthlong backpacking trip across Europe—in Cooter Brown's, in New Orleans. The grassy levee of the Mississippi stands only feet away from the door. Live oaks were nearby, persistent four-hundred-year-old gnarled sentinels. They've watched a lot happen in front of the bar over the years. They've watched strangers kiss, seen pint chuggers stumble and skin knees on the sidewalk, and observed many semesters of grinning Tulane coeds come and go, wearing cheery shirts with Greek letters. The iconic streetcars scrape and rattle their way out front, under those oaks, taking tipsy passengers home without need for designated drivers.

We sat in Cooter Brown's two decades ago, our tattered travel guide, road map, and notebook sitting on the mud-brown table, heavily carved with initials from years of such brainstorming and swigging sessions. We imprinted our initials with a Swiss Army knife, alongside the rest: *K.M.+T.B.* We talked with excitement, knowing the romantic trip overseas would be something we'd never forget. We held hands across the table, discussing how the world lay blooming before us: the palaces of Venice, sitting atop sinking swamp and fronted on one side by exotic waterways, on the other by centuries-old cobbles; the cool air of the Tyrolean Alps, where I had worked and lived during summers because of a job I had during college; the modern cities of Europe, filled with noteworthy architecture and unusually efficient railways. For our honeymoon, Europe suddenly seemed a rich and open thoroughfare, at times rough hewn, at times sleek, but always unfurled like a begging red carpet.

Our guidebook—and yes, this was back in the mid-'90s, when such things were possible—was called *Europe on $50 a Day*. The title should have been *Europe on $3.49 a Day*, because that's about how much we actually had to spend. As I remember it, the brainstorming and planning session went something like this:

Me: "Okay, we can be in Salzburg on Monday, sleep sitting up in the train station photo booth that night, then catch the train for Slovenia early Tuesday. If the picture-taking booth is occupied, we can split up and each take a bathroom stall for the night."

Tim: "That sounds fine, but what the hell is Slovenia?"

Me: "Who knows? But it's cheap—we may be able to afford sleeping indoors for a night."

Tim: "Okay, makes sense. I'm a little worried, though. I'd guess that Slovenia, wherever it is, may be a wee bit iced over in February."

Me: "I'll flip to the temperature chart in the travel guide. Hold on . . . okay, it says it here. 'Slovenia . . . February . . . low of 26 degrees, high of 39 degrees.' Perfect!"

Tim: "That's what you consider *perfect*?"

Me: "It's perfect because we'll have each other!"

And so it went. It's amazing what a dark bar and a single drink and the blur of love can do to our sense of life. Slovenia in winter? NO PROBLEM! $3.49 for food, transportation, and entrance fees? NO PROBLEM! It didn't faze us that our first month of marriage would be spent sleeping on trains, eating stale panini and frigid, uncooked beans from a can. We were together, in love, and taking a chomp out of life.

Then something happened. It took a few years, but something—not at all detectable but still real—transformed places like Cooter Brown's from being dream-hatching workshops to just some place where "single people and kids" went. During those years, the idea of Slovenia at 26 degrees also started to seem a bit . . . well . . . cold.

What happened is we had children.

When preoccupied with doling out Cheerios and dabbing calves with hydrocortisone, discussing average yearly temperatures in a country thousands of miles away while in a noisy bar is the last thing you want to do at night.

Unless, that is, you suddenly find yourself in the middle of a midlife crisis.

So now, after a worthy hiatus, I weirdly crave hanging out again in these dens of iniquity. I long to play pool badly. And throw darts that miss the board and hit the wall. I long to shout over the noise of a house band. I long to talk foolishness as if it is important, to say things that are false with complete conviction, and to have people believe it.

I want to again have someone give me the eye—even men with fifty extra pounds and receding hairlines—even for a split second. Granted, my husband gives me the eye. Sometimes he even does this when I'm sitting at home on the couch, just eating a bag of chips. But there's always a worry that his sight may be failing, so outside confirmation never hurts. No one gives me the eye on the playground or at the mini-mart. But in a bar or pub, there's occasionally someone who finds me attractive, some guy who has been imbibing since noon and does not find saddlebags and comfortable shoes to be in any way off-putting.

It's helpful that we live today just across Lake Pontchartrain from the city that supposedly boasts more bars per capita than any city in the U.S. And yes, the barkeepers of New Orleans are infamous for looking the other way when a wide-eyed sixteen-year-old Lolita walks in, sporting the latest belly piercing and smoking a Virginia Slims menthol. But even the most daring of proprietors would hesitate to admit our children when they were still studying multiplication and learning names of state capitals. That, even in the Big Easy, is just a little too young.

So we discovered—many years ago—what we affectionately call the "Bar and Grill Loophole." This loophole takes the form of a little sign, usually placed somewhere near the front door, or behind the bar. It usually reads something like this: *No one under the age of 21 admitted after 10 p.m.* When we see this, we think: Bingo! This is our kind of place.

Why, you may ask, are these words so important? They're important because the law obviously allows kids to observe the consumption of Bloody Marys and bar brands, the loud playing of music by mediocre cover bands, the inaccurate throwing of darts, the immodest dancing, and the stupid, half-baked pickup lines of a bar, as long as they all occur before ten o'clock.

Since discovering this Bar and Grill Loophole, Tim and I have been able to enjoy many evenings that resemble those of our younger days. As long as we spy the kids through the corner of our eyes—and they're not in need of a Heimlich maneuver or are not breaking too many pilsner glasses— we can pretend we're alone, for fifteen or twenty minutes, or even for an hour. We can imagine those days before we made our kids. We can imagine being free.

Sadly, when I last checked, Cooter Brown's didn't have the bar and grill loophole, but many places do. When we go to a loophole bar, the kids can make all the noise they want and nobody even notices. When they were smaller than they are now, they could call each other "poopy head." They could say to each other, "I'm smarter than you, big dummy!" as loudly and as meanly as they pleased, and no one cared; it just became a part of the din.

At some point, the kids used to busy themselves with the art of dance. They would actually dance *with* each other, a knock-kneed, loose-jointed, jerky Fred and Ginger of the elementary school set. They would cut a real rug on the linoleum, or on the squares of wooden parquet. Sometimes they would even fall down, unashamedly dust off the ole knickers, and have at it for one more round. After a while they'd tire of formality and begin to instead run quick and dizzying circles around couples on the dance floor, whizzing past matched-up pairs engaged in moves resembling . . . how do

I say it . . . screwing. They would always garner either the ire or admiration of performers on the stage. The couples, too enamored with each other, fail to notice the childish gymnastics. The kids don't notice how provocatively the grown-ups are dancing. Everyone is happy.

Here's the best part. While they'd scream and circle and celebrate, Tim and I had time alone, to talk loudly over the crappy music and enjoy a nice meal from the grill. I'd steal French fries from his plate every time he looked away. He never did find out.

Sometimes when we do a loophole outing—and we still do—we wax stupid and eloquent on the origin of the universe. Sometimes we hatch new plans, or dream some foolish dream. We talk of crazy stuff, like moving to a country where we do not speak the language, or of losing weight, or of writing a book some day.

Mostly, though, we each steal secret glances at those two kids making an annoying scene on the dance floor. We love them even more than the travel, even more than the old romance. We love their little feet in those cheap tennis shoes, making awkward moves that seem to us like poems. We love how they bump into people. We love how they think they are alone out there and wish we could be that way, too. We do not want to carve our initials into the table anymore; we want to carve *theirs*.

The best part always came when they used to stumble up to the table, tiny brows dripping with sweat, clothing askew, and interrupt to say how much fun they were having. We'd shush them, point them back to the floor, and reminisce about what a bad idea Slovenia was, smack-dab in the middle of February.

8

Chicken Soup for the Obsessive-Compulsive Soul

"A man should not strive to eliminate his complexes, but to get in accord with them; they are legitimately what directs his conduct in the world."
—Sigmund Freud

Surely you have seen obsessive-compulsive people on television and in the movies. You have seen Jack Nicholson avoid sidewalk cracks in the film *As Good As It Gets*. You have seen Leonardo DiCaprio rub his hands raw in public bathrooms, unable to get them effectively clean as the classic compulsive Howard Hughes in the movie *The Aviator*. You have probably seen *Monk*, the television detective program featuring a main character riddled with OCD. They seem to be everywhere this past decade, the weirdos who have a hard time effectively ordering their little sliver of the universe; they have a hard time getting it all "just right." They walk funny; they touch funny; they talk funny; they clean their toilets funny.

And now, as luck would have it, my mild case of OCD for once has me perfectly aligned with the times. I have never been "in fashion" in any sense of the word—until now, as regards the present overuse of hand sanitizers and toilet seat covers. It now appears that my particular brand of mental disorder is all the rage; my nutso is du jour.

It seemed when I was a child, conditions like OCD were rarely considered. My behavior, which then consisted of simple annoying bodily ticks, such as eyeblinking, fist clenching, and the making of clicking sounds that resembled mating calls of gerbils in heat, were simply disregarded as childhood habits.

But in the past decade or so, as Leo DiCaprio and a slew of other actors on television and in film portray characters taunted by the OCD demon, it seems to be almost cool. It's strange how the media seems to grab on to certain things for a time. Right now, it's the sad phenomenon of cutting.

And perhaps just as sad (from an entertainment perspective, at least) we have the reality TV hoarding of dollar-store crap and explorations of mental fetishes such as the inexplicable need to touch a light switch exactly twenty-three times before turning it off.

My particular brand of OCD weirdness is something mostly internal, forced down purposefully over years so that it won't be noticed. But based on the current media popularity of OCD, I am considering revising this approach and going full-blown. I mean, wouldn't walking in weird patterns to avoid stepping on cracks make as big a statement as would the newest designer fashions? It would definitely be more affordable. And wouldn't wearing a face mask, à la the sadly deceased Michael Jackson, really be on par with getting a trendy new pair of $300 shades? And just think of it: wouldn't you be able to get away with just about anything at all?

Innocent Bystander: "Hey, do you really think you should kill that puppy dog?"

Full-Blown Kara: "It's not me, it's my OCD!"

Okay. Now before all you crazies in the OCD lobby or whatever you have probably organized finish washing up and begin boycotting me, I will readily admit that OCD rarely causes anyone to murder puppies. It rarely causes anyone to hear the voice of Mephistopheles, or to imagine themselves to be the reincarnated ghost of Bette Davis, or to shoplift seventeen copies of *Vogue* from the local Walmart. It just doesn't do those things. It rarely causes anyone to do anything more devious than keep a running tally of every car that passes their vehicle on the interstate during a 700-mile trip; I can attest to that.

As it stands, however, my habits are rarely visible from the outside, unless, of course, you are one of the unlucky few who have witnessed me prepare a dinner involving raw poultry. Here is how it usually goes:

Me: "Hey, you just touched the chopping block I used to cut up raw chicken for the soup. *Wash Your Hands! Quick!*"

Tim: "Oh, okay."

Me: "Hey, *hold on one minute* . . . I didn't mean just run a tiny trickle of water over your hands, I meant for you to lather up, with soap. The *disinfectant* soap. If you don't we will all get salmonella poisoning! You will get a slimy little salmonella thingamajig on the remote control, and then I'll touch it, and then I'll die! And it will be *your fault!*"

Tim: "You're crazy. I'm not doing that. I rinsed. And now the towel will clean off any extra salmonella things that are on my hands."

Me: "Wait, did you just infect my towel? Now I need to get another towel! I demand a sterile work area!"

For the most part, however, this anxiety lurks below the surface as nothing more than an unmedicated personality quirk as I try to open bathroom doors with my flip-flop-adorned feet and spray unprecedented volumes of Lysol on hotel room remote controls, doorknobs, and, God forbid, toilet flusher knobs. It is all in the name of safety. Makes perfect sense, right?

There are times, however, when this anxiety gets the upper hand and seems to threaten our sense of normalcy. For instance, it sometimes comes to a head when you go to Walmart, Target, or wherever you happen to buy your favorite generic brand Doritos. Sometimes it can be hard to function in these wide open and public places because your mind wanders to the millions of spores, germs, bacteria, and parameciums that surely coat every surface. Then, your anxiety gets the better of you, and you are so wrapped up in images of the kid with tuberculosis and chicken pox that *surely* must have sat in the grocery cart immediately preceding your then eighteen-month-old child that you are barely able to shop. You think of the wiggling *E. coli* bacteria that surely clung to the consumptive child's diaper and that now creeps its way onto your own child. You rush the shopping process, vigilantly watching to make sure your son does not touch his mouth to the cart handle, which is surely one of the most infected surfaces imaginable! You are a grump, upset at your forgetfulness as regards sanitizer. You are irritable.

Me: "Dane, stop that! We do not touch our mouths to the cart. Dirty! Dirty!"

Precious Baby Dane: "No, I lick it!"

Me: "No, we do not lick it! If you lick it, I will give you a spanking!"

Precious Baby Dane: "Then buy candy! Buy me candy and I won't lick it!"

Me: "No, I *won't* buy candy, and you *won't* lick it!"

Precious Baby Dane: "You better buy it, you Fucking Mama!"

And at this point, all eyes dart to you and your dirty salmonella cart and foul-mouthed baby. Blue-haired grandmas titter in shock but pretend, for the sake of politeness, that they do not think you are a horrible woman. A stock boy giggles as he unloads the kumquats. You are mortified but will not be held hostage by a foul-mouthed baby. He will not get the candy; he will not lick the cart. And you do not sway: such is the nature of obsession.

It is interesting to note, however, how being called a Fucking Mama in front of a roomful of strangers can steel you against the myriad embarrassments that eventually come your way as a parent. After that experience, you can handle anything.

You can handle the public tantrums. You can handle broken glass (or even broken *crystal*, on a good day). You can handle the eating of large boogers while at a birthday party. You can handle kicking and screaming. You can handle dirty diaper changes as you kneel on a busy street corner.

If you have ever been publicly designated a Fucking Mama, take it from me that after that, you will be prepared when the worst happens. And you know what "worst" I am talking about, because it happens to all mamas eventually. You will be fully prepared for the inevitable question we all get at some point from our young children, while we wait in line at a checkout: "Hey, is that person a man, or a lady?"

Your youngster points to someone who seems to be Ernest Borgnine in a dress, or to someone who appears to be a teenage boy in Dickies work pants and pink nail polish. And the funny thing is, we usually don't know the answer ourselves, which is a testament to how perceptive even our babies can be. We usually answer with something like "Hey, want some candy?" or "Wanna lick the cart handle?" in an attempt to quickly change the topic.

As I age, my penchant for obsessive and compulsive behavior no longer comes with the necessity for explanations or rationalizations. I don't hide it. That takes too much work, and I don't like work. Let people think the worst—just see if I care. Let them think I am taking directions from a shadowy CIA informant, or a very friendly unicorn or whatever strikes their fancy. Let them imagine I have just escaped from a hospital. Let them think I believe myself teleported from Uranus and am struggling with a new atmosphere. Just let them think it.

Of course very few of my habits make sense. But honestly, in my tiredness I don't give a hoot if the odds of dying by paramecium are significantly smaller than the odds of death by automobile. The paramecium are everywhere. Can't say that about cars, now can you?

I don't care one whit if you think its crazy that I need to touch something with my left hand because it was touched by my right. That's just how it is. I don't actually give a hill of beans anymore if you encounter me in the ladies room at a warehouse store somewhere in suburbia and are a little frightened by my behavior at the faucet. Some things just are. *Deal with it.*

And here is the question I set before you: as we age, do we become MORE like our true selves, or do we become LESS? Seriously, really think about it. If I end up as Michael Jackson or Howard Hughes did, unable to wander the streets without a face mask and a full-on sanitization routine, would I be somehow *repressing* the little girl of my past, *or* would I finally be *setting her free*?

How, exactly, does this cookie crumble? If I had not spent all those years of my youth hiding my tics, would that compulsive little girl, with eyes-a-blinking and throat-a-clicking, finally be who she was meant to be? If I had, all along, let myself check, balance, rearrange, clean, scrape and resize without shame or fear of embarrassment, would the energy spent on hiding all this have been used somewhere better? Would I have spent it on searing haiku, or on stupid ditties that make people smile, or on a really awesome paint-by-numbers that would some day end up at Sotheby's?

Or, would letting this "real me" flourish have been a social death sentence? Had I given in from the beginning, would this mild and humorous "illness" that prevents me from making chicken soup without a meltdown have simply won? Would I be more of a mess than I am now, not only needing to wipe down remote controls, but unable to take a vacation at all? Would I not be able to eat chicken? Would my hands be raw? Would I blink thirty-seven times each minute, and count each blink? Would I feel my heart all day, and make a compulsive, beat-counting music of it, a song that would never end? Would I be unlucky and would that song be something shitty, like a tune by REO Speedwagon? That would not be good—not at all.

Are our eccentricities a baggage that we spend a lifetime trying to cast off, or are they pieces of our core, that we should let flourish?

We will never know the answer to these questions. Even if we wanted to know, there is no way to go back and get a redo. We may daydream of this when we have nothing at all to do, but in all actuality, many of us would not want to go back to our early childhoods and try again, even with the aid of hindsight. I know I probably wouldn't. As far as I am concerned, going whole hog into the tube socks and feathered hair thing is something that should happen no more than once in a lifetime.

But we *can* know this: never forget your sanitizers! Otherwise, your dirty-diapered, foul-mouthed children will publicly embarrass you one day, probably while you stand in line at a pharmacy holding your Lysol and your Xanax.

9

Suburban Tango

"Middle age is when a guy keeps turning off lights for economical rather than romantic reasons."
—Eli Cass

I haven't the foggiest idea how to do the tango. In fact, I can't do any type of official dance step. I made a brief attempt to learn some dances in the early 1990s, when country music was all the rage and there were country-western-themed nightclubs everywhere (at least here in the Deep South there were). I line-danced badly and self-consciously, pulling on my long, untucked shirt hem to cover these large hips. I awkwardly mimicked the movements of the other twenty or thirty or fifty mostly single and probably ovulating women who were on the dance floor.

I know what you are thinking it must have looked like. The only thing you could be thinking, if you know anything about the art of dance and are at all rational, is that it looked exactly like the "The Dance of the Sugar Plum Fairy" from *The Nutcracker* ballet. Granted, there was a little more clomping about, a little less finesse. There was Dwight Yoakam playing instead of Tchaikovsky. Oh, and there were no glistening fairy wings, no hair in smooth and sculptural upswept buns. Nobody even *attempted* to stand on the toe point of their cowgirl boots, the ones crafted of all man-made materials. But except for those minor differences, it was basically the same. And that's how those impromptu performers felt—like an elegant troupe, a fully synced redneck entertainment ensemble. They performed in an estrogenic frenzy for the couples who had already found each other for the night, Nutcracker Princes and girl Claras getting sloshed and ready for their one-night stands that would, in the morning, seem like dreams.

Even with my bumbling and hem tugging, every once in a while some guy would take a shine to me and take notice. I learned the two-step on one of those nights when someone took notice. He was a skinny kid, could not have been more than eighteen or nineteen years old. He had on a brown Stetson hat, Wrangler jeans, and a western-style plaid shirt with mother-of-pearl and metal snaps and elaborate decorative piping on the breast pocket. He was from somewhere in Tennessee and claimed that he was in Louisiana to ride bulls in a rodeo. It didn't matter to me whether this skinny little guy was on the up and up—what mattered is that he wanted to teach me the two-step.

And I two-stepped. I two-stepped all over his boots. I had to, because he kept calling me "ma'am."

Rodeo Cowboy: "Now you're doing it, you're getting the hang of it! Wait . . . left foot now . . . all rightie, that's it, you're catching on mighty fine now, ma'am."

Kara: "Oh, it's just because you're a good teacher. But you really don't have to call me ma'am. I'm just twenty-two."

Rodeo Cowboy: "Is that right, that you're twenty-two? Well, little miss, I'm a bit shocked because you look so young and sweet that . . . ma'am, I hesitate to confess it . . . I really thought you were some young gal, maybe roundabouts the age of sixteen, that snuck in here with an older sister and a fake ID or something like that."

Kara: "So you were interested in me because you thought I may be sixteen?"

Rodeo Cowboy: "Oh, no ma'am, I just think you looked a little lonely, like you need a little kind attention, is all . . . wait now, hold on. If you slide your right foot just like this you won't come down on my boots so much."

Kara: "Oh, you mean slide it *like this*?"

Rodeo Cowboy: "Um, when I said to slide it I meant over the floor, not over my toes, ma'am."

Kara: "Sorry, I seem to have two left feet all of a sudden. That's what happens when we ladies get old like this. When you hit about twenty everything starts falling apart, really, and by twenty-two you're such a mess you can't help but stomp around on brand-new pairs of buckskin cowboy boots when you come across them."

Rodeo Cowboy: "Yes ma'am, I'd figure as much."

My husband Tim, who I met the same year as this rodeo cowboy, thank goodness did not call me "ma'am"—but he didn't dance, either. So I never would learn an adequate two-step. Although my Nutcracker Prince had been found, I would never really dance with him. When I would try to lure him to the dance floor, he would freeze up like a real nutcracker, wooden and stiff-jointed. Even our wedding dances were stilted and self-conscious moments for us both. Some people just cannot dance if it involves placing the feet in a preordained order.

But hell if you can't learn to cut a crazy-ass rug if you don't care what you look like and put no thought to it at all! I've learned to do this over the past few years.

This mostly happened because I live in the suburbs.

Now what, you may ask, does living in the suburbs have to do with dancing? This would be a logical question. And the logical answer would be: absolutely nothing.

That's right, dancing has absolutely *nothing* to do with living in a neighborhood where fence heights and backyard deck designs need homeowners' association approval. Nobody dances the lambada in the evenings on their carefully edged lawns or jitterbugs on the sidewalk in front of the strip mall beauty parlors and drugstores. Nobody grabs a partner and waltzes around the living room during commercial breaks or while walking in the mall. Nobody wants to play the music too loud, in case a neighbor, walking by with a Labrador and plastic pooper scooper, might hear it.

Many of my years at home with children were spent living in Mississippi. Yes, I said that—Mississippi. (See? I told you I'm qualified as your guide to the wilderness.) That place offered no dancing venues. There were practically no clubs open past 11 p.m. There were no big-band orchestras or ballroom dancing to speak of. There was even nowhere with gangly pedophile rodeo cowboys.

When we first journeyed out of New Orleans and into a "planned community" exburb one hour's drive away across state lines, we defended the appeal of a lifestyle of weekend barbeques and high school football games. We saw the draw of this neighborhood of cul-de-sacs and manicured lawns that was bordered on the west by the outlying suburbs of New Orleans, on the south by the Mississippi Sound, and on the north and east by a bunch of small rural towns. It seemed a little bland, but since we had a new family to cater to, we were ready to sacrifice the unique offerings that can be found only in a city: the hustle and bustle of constant activity; the diversity of being surrounded by different types of people; the sheer variety of things to do.

We were okay that you could never watch "Performance Art" in Hancock County, Mississippi. In all truth, the fact that we could not view "Performance Art" was probably a big selling point at that time. It is interesting to ponder whether anyone else has ever had this thought when moving to the land of rural southern farms separated by planned developments. I can only imagine what a tourist brochure would have looked like if the local Chamber of Commerce had had the presence of mind to craft one specifically for us at that time:

Hancock County: Proud to Call It Home!

Do you really need to see people dressed in army fatigue–patterned leotards swing back and forth on trapezes while pretending to bleed to death?

Do you really need to pay good money to see marching bands dressed as raggedy stray cats blow bad music into tin whistles?

Do you really need to see one-man shows or self-absorbed hipster monologues about what it is like to be a lesbian-feminist-marxist in a world where people are still primitive enough to have Gunshoot Jamborees?

*Then move here, to Hancock County, Mississippi, where you will never, **ever** have to watch "Performance Art"!*

Here in Hancock County, you will enjoy all the solitude of country living with the amenities and conveniences of city life.

You will avoid the high taxes used to pay for graffiti removal and the purchase of Big Ass Beers for dignitaries.

You will never pick your nose or have to pee in a styrofoam cup while you wait in traffic, ever again.

You will never need to look over your shoulder or worry that some creep has jimmied your lock and stolen the GPS you paid an arm and a leg to have installed last spring.

You will never have to fret that your neighbors' grass is too tall or that anyone is doing anything different from anyone else.

Hancock County: Nothing to worry about—nothing to think about! Ever!

Hancock County—It's Time to Call It Home!

At the time, we were sold hook, line, and sinker on exburb life even without the aid of such an outstanding and individualized brochure. Much of this had to do with the fact that we wanted a brand-new home.

Unlike us, most friends of our age were buying or renting homes in old, transitioning areas of New Orleans. They were renovating beautiful old places upriver that were built a hundred or more years ago. These were homes with walls of solid brick and plaster, structures that had been touched and cared for by many generations, places that would stand forever and felt as if they had.

They also, at times, felt drafty and not conducive to modern life. I mean, seriously: where the heck was the built-in niche for the eighty-inch flat-screen television? Or the digital keypad for the central air and heat? Or the "light and airy" open floor plan, where one room seems to flow effortlessly into the next? How could people possibly live without these comfortable things?

Yes, I admit that those old homes have other, more subtle charms. There are cool whitewashed bricked-over fireplaces that were deemed hazards some time in the past. There are usually beautiful moldings in every room, chair rails and high baseboards and ceiling medallions so coated with multiple layers of paint that their original shapes are distorted. Those layers stand testament to how solid and loved those darn places are. There are always high ceilings and large windows with wavy old glass, and open transoms to help with air flow on those days when the sweat beads on foreheads and saturates the seersucker. And each house always has those curious parts that almost seem as artifacts of the past, such as worn porcelain claw-foot tubs and manual dumbwaiters, whatever the hell those are.

But in the end, we settled for function over form. We decided that a new home was a more comfortable environment for sitting and watching television, for supervising our kids while they crawl around on the floor and choke on lollipops, and for maintaining on fall-time weekends in fits of civic pride.

Even now that we have moved on and returned to Louisiana, I do not look back and think we had made a mistake. In fact, we recently chose another "new-ish" home just across Lake Pontchartrain from New Orleans, in a suburban neighborhood controlled by even stricter rules than we had faced in Mississippi. The benefit of a newer home instead of a historic one is that it's a lot easier to care for. What's more, you don't need a dude wearing Banana Republic skinny jeans and a chiffon scarf to help you decorate it.

Tim: "Hey, I think these shutters are looking a little faded."

Me: "Well, paint them, no big deal."

Tim: "But they are plastic, Kara. You can't paint them. It does not work that way."

Me: "Really? Well darn, when they put those things on they were blue, but now they look almost whitewashed. Why does that happen?"

Tim: "Oh, that? That's sun fade. It just happens."

Me: "Well, take them off. Throw them away and get some more down at the Home Depot."

Tim: "But damn, we don't have the budget for that. We're still paying off the expenses of replacing that hole in the drywall that happened after you leaned the broom against the wall too hard, and the debt we took on to paint the stucco so it didn't look just like the neighbors."

Me: "Yeah, I know, but that stucco painting stuff had to happen, people kept getting confused and knocking on their door instead of ours. We had to do that. So few people drive out here across the lake to see us, and we were losing half of them to the neighbors."

Tim: "Well, I guess we can throw the shutters away then. We'll just have to include 'New Shutters' on our yearly budget from now on. Ugh!"

Kara: "Just toss 'em, Timmy. And this time let's go out on a limb and paint them black—we can make some fun gossip by appearing nonconformist and dark. It will freak out the neighbors when they're walking back from the mailbox with their newest issues of the *National Review*."

In addition to easier house maintenance, which basically involves throwing away bits and pieces of your home and gluing a new piece in its place, there have been other benefits to living outside the main perimeter of the city. We are not robbed, at least not at the same rate as we were before. Our kids are safe. The public schools are of a reasonable quality. There are many bake sales.

But after a certain number of years in suburbia, be it in Mississippi or in Louisiana, even such reassurances do not hold so much sway. You begin to feel a slow and steady re-shifting of the scales. On one side is this glue-gunned house with a good school system and hollow core Masonite doors, and on the other side is . . . "Performance Art." And the side that's filled with actors in giant fake eyelashes, gorilla suits, and men dressed as Marcel Marceau twirling batons in unison begins to take on added weight. This foolish side of the scale magically accrues pounds, added to mostly by the weight of: boredom.

And no one feels such boredom more than a woman in the middle of a midlife crisis, let me tell you!

Such women often end up refusing to accept that there is no serious dancing on the north shore of Lake Pontchartrain or in Hancock County. Such women turn up the stereo very loud and crazy-ass dance for fifteen or twenty minutes every day while waiting for the school bus to drop off their kids. They will kick up their spastic legs. They will shake their butts, cellulite a-flapping. They will do some weird hops and quite a few moves that are indistinguishable from Jazzercise or some kind of aerobics. If there is enough time, the dance will often involve a bit of karaoke to songs by Pat Benatar or Harry Belafonte or Frank Sinatra: "I did it . . . *my way!*"

It is always weird; it is an "interpretive" dance, designed to convey everything that remains hidden deep within during the rounds of coffee klatches and book clubs and PTA meetings. The dance seems somehow like a burst dam. I would imagine it would be very beautiful, and scary, to witness as an onlooker; I have never been so lucky. You must have known that the suburbs have a subversive underbelly; this is it.

This dancing is basically what a tired suburban women does at home while you are walking outside, unawares, with your pooper scooper and well-trained dog. She has accepted that life involves compromises of all kind. She has accepted that if she wants to be truly entertained, she has to do it for herself. She has to feel the rebellion and the creativity and the bohemianism well up from somewhere within, instead of watching it from cheap seats in an alternative theater. And she knows deep inside, despite how much she protests and longs, that it is probably better this way; at least there are no Marxists.

Occasionally this crazy dancing gets really out of hand and turns into something that resembles a tango. These women imagine that they are with their husbands and that said husbands actually want to dance. They imagine these wooden princes come alive, if only for fifteen minutes of a waking dream. More often than not, though, during this dance these females will not have a rose between their teeth. It is quite likely that they will instead clench in their bite the permanent marker they were using just moments before, to put the kids' names on the inside of their overcoats and sweaters.

And even more rarely, the crazy-ass dancing with no official steps will take place with a mid-afternoon mango margarita in one hand, sloshing back and forth with the random movements and occasionally dripping to the wall-to-wall carpeting below. The aforementioned husband will be inadvertently watching and will say:

"Can you *please* move from in front of the TV?"

And you will say: "No. And you just don't get it. This is art—*performance art!*"

10

Pancho Villa
and the Mexican Boat People

"The only time you really live fully is from thirty to sixty. The young are slaves to dreams; the old servants of regrets. Only the middle-aged have all their five senses in the keeping of their wits."
—Hervey Allen

We do not travel much anymore.

I used to travel, quite a lot. I backpacked, many summers and a few winters as well, across Europe. Sleeping on train station floors and in inns and *pensiones*, I made my way from the tourist capitals of Europe to the alpine tundra, to the countries of the former Soviet Union that were then taking their first tiny breaths of liberty. Over the years I did everything a *traveler* is supposed to do—I did everything rich and cultural and immersive. I also did everything a *tourist* should do, including getting treated rudely by the French.

But all of that is in the past. It fell into its natural position as a thing of the past at the moment of giving birth to my son, Dane.

Obstetrician: "Okay, I think the head is crowning. Just give one big push."

Me: "Crowning? OH CRAP! No more Eurail passes!"

It was that quick, that decisive. And we have never looked back. We do, however, sometimes attempt those so-called family closeness driving trips. But to be completely honest, stopping to get souvenirs and pecan rolls at Stuckey's is not as stimulating as taking a paseo stroll along Las Ramblas, or on the Champs-Élysées, or even as awe inspiring as walking around in the Italian Home Depot in, say, Bergamo, Italy, where all the doorknobs and two by fours seem prettier because they are not American.

From time to time, though, Tim and I would find ourselves alone for a long weekend, or even for the greater portion of a week. Usually these moments of solitude used to be due to a corporate-style reward or incentive trip for Tim's job. We used to find ourselves every year or two at some resort, some highly discussed place, usually where Oprah or some such person owns a suite, and where the views look like postcards.

A few years ago we were lucky enough to visit such a resort, in a place we had never been: Cabo San Lucas, Mexico. In Los Cabos, the desert meets up with the sea in the most striking way. Endless stretches of sand and rock doggedly edge the bluest of water on one side and the dry wilderness on the other, separated by one long highway that heads north. At some points there are cacti-dotted hills that practically brush up against the waves; there are tumbleweeds parched by futile motion and relentless air; there are rock jetties extending into the energetic sea. There are small ports with clean-scrubbed white yachts, huge corporate catamarans, and generations-old wooden fishing boats with peeling paint in rainbows of vibrant color. Extravagant, tropically themed resorts stand side by side with local abodes in a nice medley of contentment. There are whales spouting seawater into the sky just yards from where fat, swimsuited American asses lounge on rented wooden beach chairs. It is heavenly.

It's heavenly, that is, when one is actually on that beach chair instead of standing around uncomfortably at functions with titles such as "Welcome Reception" and "Awards and Recognition Meeting" and "Pair of Free Designer Sunglasses—Free to All Attendees!" So, on the last day of this trip, we grew tired of the preplanned, sanitized corporate functions and decided to set out on our own. Of course we had no game plan; we just set out, designer sunglasses in hand.

Tim and I wandered the streets of Cabo San Lucas. We perused some of the pharmacies that sell drugs that would require a prescription back in the states. We longingly looked at the bottles of Prozac, Viagra, and Oxycontin. We wished we had a need or want for such contraband, as the pricing was stellar. We bought a box of penicillin, for just in case; please understand that I could not let a chance to walk on the wild side pass me by.

We made our way past the beer stands and burrito joints designed to lure in our U.S. dollars. These places held little interest; we were in search of something *authentic*. But how, exactly, does one find authentic in a town where the biggest tourist attraction is a bar that happens to be owned by Sammy Hagar?

Well, you head for the marina, that's how. I have always loved marinas— the smell, the activity, the sound of pulleys and wires clanking against masts. I love the guys cleaning stinky gray fish. I love the women hanging around on the launches, holding life preservers and coolers and stuff while the men struggle to bring their boats up out of the water. I love the crabs that run up onto the boat launch, and the barnacles that cling to the wood.

But when we get there, we discover a problem with this particular marina. The problem is that it is in proximity to the second-most popular tourist destination in Cabo San Lucas: rocks in the shape of an arch. These rocks, called Land's End, are a famous and really quite beautiful formation created by erosion. They are much photographed. You have seen them on a calendar somewhere, rest assured.

The reason this is a problem is that the "authentic" marina we were seeking was apparently not there. What was there was a tourist strip, a haven for vendors hawking their sightseeing services, hawking their tours to look at the rocks.

"I take you out, forty dollars," they'd say.

"How long is the tour? Where exactly do you go? Is it *authentic*?" I would ask.

"I take you out, forty dollars, it's *muy bien*," they would say.

"No," I would say. "Forty dollars is *mucho* dollars to look at rocks."

And finally, after having the exact same conversation several times, an earnest young man approached us with something new, something that we were sure *was* authentic:

"Boat tour, twenty-five dollars, two *personas*!" Now, my Spanish was a bit sketchy, but I was fairly sure he said twenty-five dollars for two people. And that sounded about right, it sounded like something to take a chance on. We took a look at where he stood, and there were two beautiful fishing boats behind him. They looked nice, seaworthy. Tim nodded his consent. This seemed to be a fine operation and we decided to go with it.

"You pay now," he said, as if he did not trust us. We paid him quickly in crisp American dollars, pleased with the deal.

"Now wait, boat here in *minutos*," he says.

"Oh," I say, pointing to the fishing boats behind him, "so those are not your boats there?"

"Oh, no, *señora*, our boat is *mucho* better, glass bottom."

"Okay, no problem," I say, as it sounded like we were in for quite a journey.

Within minutes, a boat pulls up, a small fishing vessel that could comfortably seat approximately eight people. It had definitely seen better days. It was wooden and was painted in the brightest of blue paint. The coating peeled from almost every surface, each scratch or flake revealing underneath it an array of different colors, each color representing a different paint job from decades past. There was a motor attached to the back, but it seemed too small for the vessel—it seemed to be designed for quiet trolling as opposed to carrying tourists into the rough waters of the Sea of Cortez.

In the center of the boat was the much-anticipated glass bottom. This bottom, designed for viewing fish underneath, consisted of what appeared to be a piece of scratched plexiglass that had been cut to fit a rectangular void in the bottom of the boat. The plexiglass was partially covered with a green algae that prohibited the viewing of anything but algae. A line of cloudy marine caulk lined the perimeter of the viewing area, filling the space between the plastic and the old wood and presumably creating a watertight seal. Water pooled in the corners of the glass; a slow seep was apparent. I wondered how much life this boat had left.

At the rear of the boat, operating this mini-motor, sat an overweight, jovial man with a huge straw sombrero atop his head. His white T-shirt was almost transparent from repeated washings—it has become almost gauze-like. You could see thick tufts of chest hair through the translucent fabric. He also wore a simpleminded grin that made me wonder if we would ever return from this journey, made me think that these damn well better be some interesting rocks we were going to see if I were going to board this vessel!

We discovered that his name was Pancho. We also learned that Pancho did not speak English. When you are about to board a tiny ages-old wooden boat with a mini-motor and nothing but caulk separating you from sharks, giant manta rays, and hypothermia, it would ordinarily be a good idea to make sure you can communicate with your guide. But a woman in the middle of a midlife crisis does not say to her husband, "Oh honey, do you think this is a good idea? Might we sink?" What she usually says is more like: "If we start to drown, you're on your own!"

And so it was.

The rock formations were actually interesting. Pancho pointed to different areas where, with a large amount of imagination, one could make out clusters of stone shaped like recognizable things and well-known characters. He pointed out "a dragon" and "King Kong" and "Scooby-Doo." When we squinted just right, we could almost see it.

Pancho had a very large gap between his teeth. I remember this gap because he never stopped smiling. It was not the smile of someone who is perpetually happy; it was the smile of someone who hadn't a clue. For a few minutes, I became concerned that Pancho was unaware that the waters had grown rough, unaware that at times the waves licked within inches of topping the sides of the boat. The waters grew rougher; I grew dizzier.

I was filled with a kind of excitement not felt in years. Usually when things happen that hold the tinge of danger, I titter and cower. But this time, an infusion of bravery appeared out of nowhere. Perhaps it was the nature of the crisis:

> midlife crisis (noun): A period of emotional turmoil in middle age caused by the realization that one is no longer young and *characterized especially by a strong desire for change.*" (www.merriam-webster.com; italics mine)

Or perhaps I simply imagined that Pancho wasn't in fact a gap-toothed, plexiglass-caulking fisherman, but was, instead, the reincarnated spirit of Pancho Villa.

In either case, we set around a large formation of rocks that had a small beach. The entire island was approximately the size of a football field. Somehow, I do not now know how, Pancho conveyed that this was a nude beach. Naturally, we started to scan the scene, in an effort to look for naked people. I figured if I were going to meet my maker by sinking next to some Scooby-Doo-shaped rocks with Pancho Villa, why not top it off by having my last moment spent looking at some buff Mexican sunbathers?

My husband craned his head to catch a much-anticipated glimpse, but there were no naked sunbathers. There was no one on this beach but a gang of fully clothed men, hanging out on the sands. They did not have a boat with them, or even a few kayaks. They were just sitting there on this island.

When one chances upon a large gang of men on an island beach next to King Kong–shaped rocks in the Sea of Cortez, one would generally expect said men to be dressed as pirates or castaways or some such. That would be my educated guess. But these men were different—they carried iPods.

It is unusual to find a random gang of men with iPods and cell phones in their hands, but no way to transport themselves out of the ocean to do so much as grab a Gatorade. I wondered—how long had they been there? What were they drinking? What were they listening to on their iPods? What did they do when they were in the middle of listening to "La Bamba" and the iPod charge died? And most important—why did they wear clothes?

As these questions rumbled through my mind, Pancho indicated that he would beach the boat to pick up some of these men. "*Mis amigos*," he said. His friends.

The *amigos* began to board the boat. A few of them were old and salty—you got the feeling they had visited this island, and boarded Pancho's boat, quite a few times. Two of them were young and swimsuited. A few wore blue jeans and sports shirts. There was no rhyme or reason to the constellation of personalities that climbed aboard.

As each person boarded and the boat seemed to dip deeper into the water, I said aloud to my husband, "Wow, he has a lot of friends, and they are *all* getting on this boat!" When everyone was in place, we had roughly fifteen people aboard a boat that had been designed to hold eight. We sat thigh to thigh, and you could smell the funk of the sea and the faux coconut of suntan oil. The boat was burdened—the caulk seemed to groan.

How, oh how, I wondered, would this trolling motor transport us all across the high seas? And if it could not, were any of those cell phones waterproof?

We ply the tremendous waves slowly, a mist of water coming over the bow, waves lapping within inches of where we sat. The best part: there were no life jackets on board! Not a single one! But does a woman in the middle of a midlife crisis panic about such trifles? No. What she does is she asks Pancho in broken Spanish when we will get back to the marina. And what does he say? Why, of course:

"After I catch dinner."

Or, at least that's what I *thought* he said.

And he wasn't kidding. Seemingly unaware of the fact that there were two paying customers onboard, Pancho abruptly stopped the motor and began to unfurl a very long fishing line that was wound around a spool. Attached to the end was a small wooden lure that appeared to be as old as the boat we sat in and—I am not joking here—a large rusty wrench. We watched in horror as the boat rocked violently back and forth in the waves and Pancho balanced precariously, lowering the wrench and hook into the depths. The line was *very* long and it seemed to take forever. *Los Amigos* were unfazed. Someone texted on an iPhone while Pancho wrangled with his dinner.

What he pulled up from the depths, after ten minutes of fighting with fishing line cutting into his palms, was nothing less than the kraken! Or, so it seemed to a woman accustomed to *normal* seafood, meaning seafood that does not look like it came from a horror film. What he pulled from the water was a creature with huge tendril-like tentacles, writhing and grasping out at the ungraspable air to which they had never before been exposed. It was a huge squid, difficult for one man to hold on his own, measuring approximately four feet in length. It had a single beak-like black claw and two huge, dark, sad eyes that I cannot forget.

You would think that this sea monster would be enough to feed Pancho's family members, even if they did have large appetites. But no, we had to bear the rocky waters, the dizziness, and the texting, through four rounds of squid fighting. He even had Tim help pull one up out of the depths.

So, on this short weekend in Mexico, I felt briefly reborn. I had fed, for at least a moment, the *"strong desire for change"* described by Merriam-Webster. It was definitely a change to risk life and limb on the high seas with thirteen Mexican men (some wearing Speedos) and four very sad, captive cephalopods.

But it also kind of felt a little bit like old times. It felt a little like setting on foot up a hill somewhere in northern Italy, illegally trespassing over somebody's land, just to touch a crumbly and very beautiful wall you had spied from the roadway. It felt a little like careening, out of gas, down an entire mountain in the Alps, hoping that you would make it to the bottom and that an Esso station would be waiting there. It felt a little like having German shepherds, big smelly dogs snarling through flimsy muzzles, sniff your slumbering face as their Parisian cop master says in heavily accented English: "You can't sleep here! No sleeping in train stations!" It felt like old times. So, it seems that at times the *"strong desire for change"* may simply mean a change *back*, a change to doing what you used to do.

Thank goodness for Cabo San Lucas, and for Pancho, and for those stupid Scooby-Doo rocks. Thank goodness the caulk held. Thank goodness the sea monsters became our victims before we became theirs. It turned out to be the best twenty-five *dolares* that we had ever spent.

Of course, that night we had calamari for dinner, outside, under the stars.

11

This Ain't No Boogie Wonderland

"Growing old is mandatory; growing up is optional."
—Chili Davis

I hated cell phones; it took me a long while to get onboard. The technology has now, of course, expanded to include all manner of smart phones, wristband web portals uglier than the calculator watches nerd boys wore in 1984, and even glasses where the Internet streams in front of your eyes constantly, so as to block out petty annoyances, for instance, reality.

My dislike began many years ago, about the time that these phones shrank from the size of a brick and began to be widely used in restaurants and movie theaters to annoy people.

I made the conscious decision to hate them while sitting in the airport one day long ago. I was next to this guy who paced back and forth in his pricey pinstriped business suit and French cuffs and spoke words into his portable communication device as loudly as was humanly possible. He glanced around sideways continually to see who was noticing:

"Yeah, I will be able to work on that, since I'm flying *first class* I'll be *comfortable* enough to get some work done . . . I'll look at it and see if it meets with my approval . . . uh-huh . . . no, I want to be able to approve it first . . . uh, no, I can't, I will be seeing my therapist tomorrow, am having a major breakthrough right now and don't want to miss this session . . . oh, that thing? Yeah, it's black tie, so make sure *my assistant* has my clothes ready on time."

You all know this guy. You have all *heard* this guy, loudly talking about stock trades and snazzy vacation resorts as he not so subtly searches the eyes of strangers for approval. He is the very same guy who pretends to know things about wine because he visited Napa once and took a tasting seminar. He also owns some idiot thing he calls a "smoking jacket." But the difference between you and me is that you were not dissuaded from getting a cell phone by this guy.

I decided then and there that cell phones were a source of evil. I hated the people who used them (umm . . . that would be basically everyone at this point), and believed that a desire to own one indicated some sort of deep-seated feeling of self-importance. My sensible line of thinking: who really needs to be *that much* in touch with people? Whose job is *that* pressing that they need to have instant communication always at the touch of the fingers, much in the way that the president has to always cart around that red nuke phone in its aluminum suitcase (by the way, is the red nuke phone still in a suitcase, or is it now in a little cell pouch that clips to the waist of a Secret Service guy? Just wondering).

To be honest, I have never really found other people to be all that interesting that I could not wait until getting off the toilet to talk to them. Do we need to have an instant connect to others while we clip our toenails, or stand in the checkout line at Bed Bath & Beyond? Or, as a friend felt the need to do to me once, while taking a lavendar-scented bubble bath? Why is it now considered socially appropriate to have a conversation while your talking partner urinates? And what, pray tell, are the new social protocols as regards this? Are we supposed to politely ignore the tinkly special effects and toilet flushes, much as one would politely ignore a belch that innocently escaped at table? Or, are we to mention it, saying something like "Hey, you're a multitasker, I like that!" Or, is it now some kind of status symbol to believe oneself too important now, too busy with pressing things, to take a diarrhea break without simultaneously closing a sales deal? It may be just an urban legend, but I have heard tell also of those (including you, no doubt) who take it even further, actually upping the ante and surfing the Internet on thin laptops while using public restrooms. Is our time so precious that we now need to download spreadsheets while nature calls?

And another thing about that cell phone guy in the airport: personally, when I go to a black tie affair and need an assistant to get my clothing ready, it goes more like this:

Me: "Hey Timmy, can you grab that black dress out of the back of the closet?"

Tim: "I'm getting ready. Can't you do it yourself?"

Me: "No, I am busy waxing my upper lip again, so I need your help."

Tim: "Oh, okay . . . Are you talking about this flowered housecoat thing? Oh no, that's not it, that's the one you wore when you painted the baseboards because your jeans were too tight to kneel down all day. Hold on a sec, I'll find it."

All we really want to do while sitting in the airport, waiting for a flight to Disney World, is mindlessly stare off into the precious semi-silence. We want to enjoy the low rumble of jet engines and the benign clackety-clack of cheap luggage wheels over linoleum. We know that within a few hours "It's a Small World" will be circulating in the old noggin for days, bouncing off the inside walls of our craniums like an insidious bubbled screensaver. We know that we are shortly in for a large dose of magic, with the Play button stuck on repeat. What we do not want to do, right at that moment, is listen to anyone talk about their therapy.

If I talked in public about my therapy, it is *very* doubtful anyone would be all that interested. There would be no revelatory "breakthrough" or anything to share with strangers on a concourse. If you sitting there, minding your business and waiting for your flight, and overheard my urgent phone call about therapy, it would probably sound something like this:

"Yeah . . . yeah . . . I feel pretty fat right now, it may just be the period . . . yeah . . . well, when I get like this I just eat cheesecake and I feel better . . . yeah, I knew you'd understand . . . "

Somehow, in the age when not having an iPhone has become tantamount to living without electricity or penicillin, I had been able to maintain this anti-phone position for many, many years. Even when we had young children and drove an oil-leaking rattletrap of a car, I justified not having one because "Everyone else in the world has a cell, so if I ever break down on the side of the road and need help, I'll just ask someone if I can borrow theirs."

And what manner of poetic justice would you imagine befalling someone with such a plan? What would you imagine would happen to make me regret this decision? Well, here's what happened: absolutely nothing. The car does not break down on a lonely, dark highway filled with rapists, pedophiles, and gangsters in the middle of nowhere. The kids do not asphyxiate on lollipops while we are at the park. We never do need to call 911. And I am able to shop, every time, without calling home to ask urgent questions about toothpaste and ravioli. I survive just fine.

So you may wonder what eventually compelled me, a few years ago, to cave and buy a phone. The answer is that there really is no answer, except to say that it made me feel a little like a teenager to hold it.

Still today, not much meaningful communication takes place on this Android thingamajig that I still don't understand how to fully operate. I don't do much texting, and of course we all know that real communication can only take place within the confines of a text. But I use it sometimes for work—setting up interviews and whatnot, since I work now as a freelance journalist—and like to hold it when feeling particularly forty-something-ish. Unlike most people, I try not to obsess on a theme for the screen display (I have chosen one that looks playful, yet not immature, despite my secret inner desire to use a photo of The Fonz). I always squint my eyes when looking at it, lifting up my glasses to see or even switching to a new pair, further deepening the trenches of wrinkles that have begun to insinuate themselves at my temples. I attempt to see the tiny letters and numbers and Missed Calls messages on the miniscule screen, but sometimes it's all just too stressful and I pretend to myself in denial that no calls ever came in.

I try not to act visibly befuddled. I try not to seem like my parents were with their first microwave (they took an actual class in how to use it). I don't do fancy apps but will play mahjong while waiting in a car line outside the school or while in a waiting room. That game, I can handle.

Basically, I carry a smart phone so as to somehow appear "with it," but never actually give out the number.

Quite seriously, though, why would anyone want people phoning them while they drive to PTA meetings, or while they check out the fat and calorie content of a box of Oreos? Wouldn't it be distracting? Also, it would just make me think of how the people calling are surely being rude to the other people in the theater, or at the next booth in the restaurant, or, more important, on the concourse. I do not like to be an enabler.

As if the smart phone situation were not bad enough, a few years before I got the phone, I also capitulated and bought an MP3 digital music player (wow, that sounded geeky). The day I did it, I sought out a salesperson who was older than I was. I wanted to be sure that my squinting at the stupid thing would not make me feel a little antiqued. An older person would *get* all the squinting, would understand that I was not trying, in some creepy-mom way, to flirt with them. Old people know the difference between bedroom eye squints and "I can't see shit" squints, you can be sure of that.

So I bought the thing. I actually did something crafty and made a fuzzy crocheted MP3 case. I actually remember adding "Crochet MP3 pouch" to my to-do list. You know the list, the one that has stuff on it like "Put *Sixteen Candles* in Netflix Queue" and "Do Something About Thighs" and "Don't Forget to Feed the Kids."

I had been so resistant to digital music. I still sometimes listen to vinyl record albums on the dusty old turntable bought at age fifteen. The albums are from twenty-five or thirty-five years ago, but the music on them is much better than most of what's around today. The old collection includes a wide array of genres and styles. There's quite a bit of Bowie, including all his great albums, a picture disk with his svelte self on it, and something weird where he reads the writings of Bertolt Brecht; a few albums by Queen, including their *Greatest Hits*, which I literally wore down by playing so many times; some dabblings in U2; everything by the Cure; that one album by Led Zeppelin that I'd always play just to hear "Kashmir"; and practically every record ever made by Duran Duran, including Japanese twelve-inch singles with wacky Japanese fonts that, when I played them, made the music seem somehow exotic (it isn't). I still sometimes spin vinyl on that turntable, convinced until recently that a twelve-inch picture disk, even played with a twenty-year-old nub of a needle, is better than digital stuff any day.

Back then there was a big, colorful album cover to look at, and a dust sleeve with lyrics to read as the record turned. There were always sexy or silly or behind-the-scenes pictures of the bands on there, and a list of producers and managers and girlfriends they wanted to thank. There was a bulk to it. There was something to hold, something to rest on your abdomen when you lay back in bed to experience the music. It had been difficult enough to transition to CDs in the 1990s, what with their miniature versions of album covers, encased in brittle, antiseptic plastic. But a digital player was something altogether different: what, exactly, was there to look at with an MP3 player? A *digital screen*? Would you really lie dreamily on your bed and hold on to *that*?

A major part of my resistance had also been: I couldn't figure out what the hell a digital music player was. Although I can work my way around a computer in normal ways, technical things had never been my forte. How it all worked was an enigma. How did the music get in there? Where did it come from? Were you supposed to buy the CD first and then transfer it, or did you just simply buy the digital version somewhere online? And does anyone even listen to entire albums anymore, or is it all about individual songs? And the most important, and pressing, question I had encountered in all of this: what the hell is a Skrillex?

Once it was all explained by a baby-boomer salesperson who was not taken aback by my medieval worldview and mild Gen X squints, I gave it a go. Once the realization struck that I could go anywhere without hassling with a big stack of CDs, I was willing to forgo those powerful feelings of nostalgia and at least give this thing a try. What the hell. I am now adventuresome in this way.

I soon experienced the benefits of going digital. No more organizing jewel cases! No more swerving on the road and almost hitting stray cats while trying to find the right disc, which was always in the wrong case! No more CDs or records that were unplayable due to scratches! The thing was growing on me.

It must be said that this little MP3 thing, my little buddy, is more than I expected. I know most of you listen to music on your phones, but I'm too befuddled to figure that out and stick with carrying two separate items in my purse. It's my own little way of not giving in too much.

But I've adjusted. Digital music is almost like having your own teeny-tiny personal DJ in your pocket. When he uses the Shuffle feature, he mixes everything just right and never makes annoying comments between the songs. And how, oh how, does he know how to find your top thousand favorite songs and somehow know the exact moment to play each one?

As an added bonus, he also wears the coolest disco-era satin pants (heck yeah, my DJ is over-the-top!). He is of the gold chain and chest-haired variety. He is a little short, like me. He would need to be, to fit in my pocket. Sometimes he looks a little like the mustache guy in Hall and Oates, only with a little more pizzazz, a little more *Saturday Night Fever* shimmer around the edges. When he spins tunes, he repeatedly touches my soul inappropriately and temptingly runs his hands along the sides of my dancing shoes (when he does this I am a little embarrassed for him, as he really is going a bit too far).

Little DJ Buddy: "Put on these dancin' shoes, hot mama, you know you want to!"

Me: "But white ladies over forty can't dance, especially in that kind of heel!"

Little DJ Buddy: "True, but when you get your groove on, girl, you are just sixteen."

For some reason, this idiotic talk makes sense. I wonder often if he has slipped me a mickey, put a little something intoxicating in my decaf. And then I see it, clear as day: *life* has slipped me a mickey.

When I walk around my home or the neighborhood or the shopping center listening, it seems I'm not some fat middle-aged house frau after all. What I am, especially when lying quietly on the couch with eyes closed and volume turned up high, is a cool young kid, a fan of '80s New Wave music. I am transformed. When my eyes are closed in this digital world, my hair is dyed hot pink and often styled into a tall, stiff Mohawk. I have on turquoise and red eye shadow, blocky and in bands upswept toward the temples. I am very skinny. I am someone who digs music a lot and obsesses on a beat as much as I do lyrics that hit home. I am someone who can cry about things beautiful but somehow still be able to pretend—to those I don't trust—that I'm unaffected. And all through it, I'm waiting for my first kiss.

Then sadly, when I need to open my eyes, when the inevitable fight erupts between the kids over who was cheating at some game or another, or by dog barks because our mutt had not been let out all afternoon, my imagination fizzles. I fidget with the tiny buttons to shut the thing off, and this is always when DJ Buddy chimes in:

Little DJ Buddy: "Hey, hot mama, what you doin'? You gotta be kidding; you aren't really putting me in that ugly-ass crochet case again, are you?"

Me: "Have to. I need to settle a fight or the kids will kill each other."

Little DJ Buddy: "*And?*"

Me: "And I will have a problem on my hands."

Little DJ Buddy: "Aw, no such thing! Here, play this. It's "Girls Just Wanna Have Fun." It'll do the trick. Or here, I know which one always works on you—"Boogie Wonderland." Let me play that one, just switch it into the Shuffle mode and I'll call it up, okay?"

Me: "I wish I could . . . but the kids need me . . . and this ain't no boogie wonderland. This is the Gulf South."

And this is how it ends every time, the spell broken, the intoxication worn off.

My little buddy gets put away in his most effeminate of carrying cases, the one he hates, and I think: that thing was totally worth the purchase price.

But I do wonder sometimes why I would even *want* to be that pink-haired girl. Why, I ask you, would I *ever* want to be plunked smack-dab into a life without responsibility or schedules or stupid insurance premiums? Why would I want to listen to songs with idiot lyrics and cliché hooks? Why, oh why, would I want to be swept up into a childish abandon and lofted high inside a cherry-scented wind of nostalgia to a place of *stupid* emotion? Why would I want to be lifted up and back into a crappy junior home-coming dance, or a sloppy and ineffective flirt next to a smelly hall locker? *Why?* Isn't it enough now to be a beloved wife and a fair-to-middling mom? Isn't it full enough to be a fairly good and honest person, and to know that I have a humor about me, or to know that my kids are gifted with all kinds of love? Isn't it enough to know that if I am lucky, there are still forty or fifty years of life ahead of me, forty or fifty years of memories and opportunities and chances to make a serious impact?

Nah. Not really.

12

Screwed by the Warranty

"Life begins at 40—so do fallen arches, rheumatism, faulty eyesight, and a tendency to tell a story to the same person, three or four times."
—William Feather

When we reach the midpoint of life, our bodies begin to fall apart. And by fall apart, I do not mean that at certain time of the month, we can no longer wear our skinny pair of jeans. What I mean is: there are unusual bulges where there had never been any before, bulges that are apparently setting up shop for the duration. They are fatty unwelcome squatters unpacking their bags in your belly and hanging up their family pictures inside your hips. They are not moving out anytime soon. They are bulges so large they look like potatoes or candied yams or old inner tubes growing under your skin.

Our eyes seem to get smaller as our asses get fatter. Thank goodness. It is probably because we have begun squinting. Some of us middle-aged types have eyes that no longer see the words on Advil bottles or smart phones without dime store reading glasses or bifocals. Honestly, it's probably a blessing to have the vision obstructed during this aging process. It would be pretty darn hard to have to witness all of this in startling high def.

Even worse, some of us will start to fall down occasionally when we roller-skate. Or to breathe hard. Others of us have random pains in the knees after watching too much television and eating a bagful of sweets.

When all this, or even some of this, starts to happen, we basically have reached what I call the "screwed by the warranty" stage.

We all know what the screwed by the warranty stage is, as we have probably all owned a brand-new car at least once. When we buy the snazzy new thing, replete with the fresh car smell of polyvinyl chloride as it outgases (mmm, sniff it up! Delicious!), it runs like clockwork. This car is kept clean inside—it is dusted, sprayed with copious protectant, and the Cheetos crumbs are vacuumed out bimonthly. It is parked way, way out in the parking lot, where it cannot receive body dings from asshole drivers in old cars who park too close and open up their doors just a little too wide.

Time passes. The telltale smell of new car dissipates, and the vehicle begins to reek instead of the Burger King bag filled with dried-up onions. Round-about this time, we reach the point where we no longer feel the need to park a football field's distance to the superstore entrance. We think: "What difference will a few dings make to this car? It is getting a little older, anyway. It still runs like a thoroughbred, but its days of looking impressive are over."

Early on in our lives, perhaps during our twenties, we treat our bodies the same way. We rarely check under the hood, because, damn, this thing runs! We do not bother with too many oil changes. Our knees feel fine. We have trust in the timing belts and the starter and feel that the gas tank could never, ever rust. We leave trusty ole Betsy exposed to the elements.

Now why, exactly, would we choose to do that? Well, probably for the only reason that could possibly make any sense: because we believe age spots, wrinkles, arthritis, sleep apnea, hypertension, and diabetes are things that only happen to *other people*. We see ourselves as forever young, Dorian Grays who are caught in a perpetual spring, impervious to the sun and ravages of time and effects of luxury. We think we will be all souped up and shiny forever.

We go along in this fashion for some time, skipping the ten-point tune-ups, focusing instead on having kids, careers, and crème brûlée. We are not worried about maintenance—we can always go that extra mile.

And then there is the creep of age—the reality of that fourth decade—and the inevitability of getting screwed by the warranty.

We all know how warranties work. Some auto manufacturers offer elaborate bumper-to-bumper deals as enticements to buy, and others have extended warranties available for a fee. But the norm is usually a standard warranty that covers you for up to 36,000 miles. That means if a hose breaks or a belt pops or the A/C runs a little warm, you would just take it on in to the dealership; it would be taken care of.

But nothing ever happens. You drive ten times to grandma's, seven hundred miles away. You push your metal chariot to the limit a few times, late at night on a barely patrolled open road, just so you can see what happens. You let her idle too much; you keep her running just for the A/C while you wait for the next available teller. You always break hard. You crank that sucker up every day at 6 a.m. for several years. You ride her around to baseball practices and weekend parties and Sunday drives. You always forget to warm her up.

Even after all of this, no parts fall off; no noises rattle around; no oil leaks out to leave marks on the driveway. Yes, you did forget once to check the rearview mirror and accidentally backed into that pole in the Chevron station parking lot. And yes, your child did, on a Tuesday afternoon one day in the fall, put a rock through the driver's side window when he was learning to use the new slingshot. But as far as the engine goes, it just purrs.

This is also how *we* are, going along through life in our twenties and early thirties. We're marred only by a C-section scar, or an ankle break from skiing. We are scarred only by unforeseens that strike in the night like occasional slingshots through the glass. We trip while going after a ball. We get a tooth conked out when our bratty cousin pushes us off a diving board, but just not forcefully enough or with any warning. We accidentally poke the whites of our eyes with a mascara wand we tried to use while also driving somewhere on I-55. Oftentimes when we are young, these telltale tolls on our body are just as often signs of lives of derring-do and success as they are marks of deterioration.

And then, something changes.

For the car owner, at around the two-year-and-nine-month mark, this will happen:

Tim: "What's in the mail today?"

Me: "Just a bunch of junk mail is all. No, wait . . . we also got something about the warranty on the Mazda—it's about to expire."

Tim: "Time flies. It seems like just yesterday we got that car."

Me: "I know, time flies. So, what do we want to do about this? Will we get the extended warranty?"

Tim: "Heck no. That's a great car, it has . . . oh, maybe 250,000 miles of life in it. And it's Japanese, besides. Japanese cars don't have problems, they are well made. Great engines in those babies."

Me: "But what if something goes wrong? A car can't last forever, can it? Don't things wear out?"

Tim: "I have faith in Mazda. Things wear out, but it will take a lot longer than three years."

So the warranty expires.

And then, exactly three years and thirteen days after you bought the car, you get into it one morning and the thing just won't turn over.

That, my friend, is getting screwed by the warranty.

You are not actually getting screwed by Mazda, as these were the agreed-to terms. *Of course* you know that the thing was expired and that you would be left to pay for your own deteriorations and, God forbid, breakdowns. *Of course* you know that if anything went wrong, it would be a very expensive proposition. *Of course* you know that you aren't getting screwed by the guys on the assembly line who expertly put on the bolts in sheer boredom and applied the windshield wipers as if they were on autopilot. And *of course* you know that you aren't even getting screwed by the rain or the hail or the dry air that rots the hoses and gaskets.

But doesn't it kind of *feel* like you are?

There are times when it seems almost certain that all these parts, these hoses and gaskets and rubber belts, and joints and cells and muscles and ganglia, had come with a clear expiration date. It seems like the windshields and scalps and skin and tits and lugnuts all have a secret time stamp, just as a gallon of milk has a tiny purple date typed on its side. I have always felt sure that the expiration date of the inner workings was somehow magically set to pass roundabout the time the warranty expires.

Just as with a car warranty, my body is starting to mail out some last reminders: *"Expiration: soon!"* Although menopause is hopefully still a few years away, it seems the last vestiges of youth—vitality, smooth skin, energy, metabolism, *glow*—are already becoming a thing of the past. When we are young, we have things to fall back on, much as the auto owner has the backing of a warranty to help him out of a bind. Feeling a little fat? No problem, just take a few caffeine pills, skip dinner for a week, and the five pounds melt off. Twisted your ankle playing tennis? No big deal, just stick an ice pack on there, and in two days it's good to go. We can count on something to get us out of a bind and to tune everything back up tight.

But now those days are over. The warranty is about set to expire—I have received notice.

The signs of this creep start slowly, innocuously. There is one pill we need to take that we didn't need before. There is this little accommodation we need to make to get a good night's sleep that had not been necessary a year ago. We are starting to need to add extra oil to the engine, now and again. There are some soot stains on the tailpipe.

And then comes the night when you realize for sure that the warranty has run out. It goes something like this:

Me: "Okay, done taking out my contact lenses. Let's go to bed, I'm tired."

Tim: "Hey, since you're still out of bed, can you hand me those glucosamine and chondroiten tablets? I forgot to take them."

Me: "No problem."

Tim: "Hey, I hate to ask you this, but could you please put your vaporizer on a lower setting? It wakes me up all night."

Me: "Are you kidding? Your stupid breathing machine is a constant annoyance, you are such a hypocrite!"

Tim: "Come on, you know that machine keeps me from snoring. Are you trying to say you want me to go back to snoring?"

Me: "Well, no, but . . . I . . . look, couldn't you at least take that stupid tooth-grinding guard out of your mouth while we talk about this?"

Tim: "I will only take it out to talk to you if you wipe off that stupid face mask and take off the Crest White Strips! Don't you think they are just as distracting?"

Me: "Hold on. Look, let's just agree that we are both sometimes annoying at night, but we need to make accommodations for each other."

Tim: "You're right. We're just acting grumpy tonight. I am so sorry. Here, take your lumbar support pillow and go to sleep. I turned on your electric blanket, so you should be able to sleep pretty well tonight, especially with that big melatonin you took earlier."

Me: "You are so sweet, I am sorry for yelling at you. I hope your ankle brace does not fall off again tonight. Good night."

Tim: "Good night, my babes."

(silence)

Tim: "Hey, are you awake?"

(silence)

Tim: "Hey, wanna make some love?"

And what, pray tell, does a woman on the cusp of middle age *do* when she realizes the warranty is up? *What does she do?*

She high-tails it to the mall. She spends an afternoon at the Estee Lauder counter. She tries stuff on. She buys herself a fancy new set of rims. Not just everyday rims, but six-spoke chrome light-ups.

She also gets body work done; she has them pull out the dent from that pole-hitting incident. She nips; she tucks; she cuts; she scrapes; she plucks; she pays. She calls the glass guy to fix the slingshot window, and she sounds really pissed off when he answers the phone.

Damn straight if she ain't gonna fix up the outside of that warranty-less sucker! Even if it struggles to turn over, even if it sputters and leaks oil and the radio plays nothing but religious stations and some broken-up old Perry Como shit, it damn well better be looking good sitting in the driveway.

The airbag deployment system may be broken and the brake pads about to go out. But she'll be damned if anybody, aside from her husband, ever needs to know about any of this.

13

Supergirl in a Kayak

"Youth is the period in which a man can be hopeless. The end of every episode is the end of the world. But the power of hoping through everything, the knowledge that the soul survives its adventures, that great inspiration comes to the middle-aged."
—G. K. Chesterton

On August 29, 2005, Hurricane Katrina, the worst natural disaster to occur in United States history, hit us like an immense and clarifying wind. The single eye of this storm, a Cyclops huge and mad and crying floods, passed directly over us. At the time, we lived an hour east of New Orleans, on the Mississippi Gulf Coast. We were only a few miles from ground zero—Waveland—where a thirty-foot wall of water and debris covered every bit of ground for miles inland, for as far as the eye could see and much farther than even the broadest of minds could imagine.

Who would have thought that four and a half feet of this water would find its way into a house sitting twenty feet above sea level? We returned the morning after the storm to find the first story destroyed by water laced with fertilizer, chemicals, mud, oil, and remnants of things that used to be alive. Parts of the neighborhood were barely recognizable, and several longleaf pines, trunks partially wind-stripped of bark, were crashed into our roof. When we first approached, a snake dropped dramatically—almost Hollywood blockbuster–style—from the rooftop, draping wildly and momentarily around Tim's shoulders, like a serpentine stole. The rat snake had no doubt found his way to the roof in an act of survival from the rising waters, much as many humans had also done.

After returning home, we lived in what can best be described as squalor, the first three weeks of which were spent without electricity, running water, warm food, flushing toilets, or sleep. While the standing water—and horror—unfurling in Orleans prevented our friends and family in the city from returning, homeowners on the coast were enmeshed in this new third world immediately.

For relief, we'd chat with the neighbors, both ones we knew and ones we didn't. We'd spot them outside as they carted their sopping memories out to the curb, as they put high school yearbooks, and Santa Claus decorations, and old *Tiger Beat* magazines, and proud college diplomas, and baby pictures, and hard-earned marching band letterman jackets that (somehow) didn't win them any chicks, and tattered copies of Eisenhower biographies, and Victoria's Secret negligees, and never-used bread machines, and ecru-colored beaded wedding dresses, and dirty videos still on VHS, and Hewlett-Packard CPUs, and collectible Beanie Babies, and favorite pairs of jeans from The Gap into ever-growing piles near the road.

We talked to people who drove up to home-sweet-home and found nothing but a blank slab of concrete, wiped clean, with no discernible possessions left behind in the landscape to salvage. We heard of entire homes floating away from their original locations, like the one we saw that landed atop railroad tracks in Bay St. Louis, *Wizard of Oz*–style. We heard that families no more than three blocks away punched holes in roofs with axes and hammers to climb outside, to where there was less water and more breathable air. We also heard myriad unproven tales, never officially reported but now held as truth in local lore: herds of deer, seen running only steps ahead of flood waters; alligators found in the Garden Center of the Waveland Kmart, along with waterlogged employees who had sought shelter among the cheaply made garments and ramen noodles; a local who survived, despite spending eight hours naked, hugging an oak tree while wind sandblasted skin raw.

When finished sharing daily gossip, we'd get back to dismantling what remained of the first floor of our house. We ripped soggy drywall from the studs and frogs would jump out, bounding into our living room with the wild abandon of the recently freed. It was surreal. A few times, when we tired of sponge baths with dirty face towels and a gallon of FEMA water, we'd take part in public cleaning at a local well, where water poured continuously from a makeshift PVC spigot. Our neighbors were there, wearing swimsuits and holding slivers of soap and scrubbing their armpits and private areas in front of complete strangers.

When all was said and done, we considered ourselves lucky: we were still there, unlike the many who had not survived. This made us grateful for the spigot, grateful for the frogs.

What, you may wonder, does Hurricane Katrina have to do with a midlife panic that was not even due for several years? Well, here's what it had to do with it—the weeks following this disaster are when I discovered that, despite obvious slacker tendencies, I could be like a super hero. If I wanted to. If I *needed* to.

This is not to suggest that I suddenly developed a spitting-image resemblance to Lynda Carter, or developed pointy breasts and began flying in invisible jets, wearing wrist cuffs to deflect small arms fire. And I'm not unique; this happened to a lot of us, the ones who decided—for better or worse—to not just crouch in a corner, shivering. What I'm explaining is that an inner wherewithal rose to the surface that I had never formerly possessed or recognized. I discovered a power that made me not so afraid of stuff anymore. I suddenly had the superpowers—deserved or not—of someone who had nothing to lose.

(As an aside, just a few years ago I learned that the "real" name of the comic book hero Supergirl—when she's wearing her street clothes—is actually Kara. Her Bruce-Wayne-Peter-Parker-Clark-Kent name is Kara. Like me. Hmmm.)

When a woman reaches her forties, a touch of fearlessness can go a long way. We all need a tad. A tidbit. A smidgen. Before the storm—before my strength, and my values, and my lifestyle, were really tested—would I have had the confidence to wear six-inch-high platform flip-flops in public (and especially with long toenails)? Would I have bought my first pair of false eyelashes? Would I have the bravery to tell you all: yes, I love to lick the icing off a cupcake and then throw the cake part away, and *what of it*?

I also adopted a type of grace under fire that had always lain hidden. In the past, when stressful events had happened, they usually went something like this:

Me: "Dane, you've been a good boy today. Do you want a lollipop?"

Dane: "Yeah, mama, I want candy!"

Me: "Okay, be careful now when you eat that, make sure not to talk or jump around while eating it, and always hold on to it when you're sucking it."

Dane: "Okay Mama, but I have to know, which is your favorite movie, *Toy Story* or *Toy Story 2*? My favorite is . . . Aaagh . . . Gasp . . . Gasp . . ."

Me: "He's choking! He's choking! Dane, I told you to hold on to it and not talk! It's stuck in his throat! What do I do? Call 911? But the cordless isn't charged. See? I knew we should have kept that old corded phone, just for emergencies! I don't know how to do a tracheotomy! Aren't you supposed to use a disposable pen to do an emergency tracheotomy? I don't even have that, you darn kids keep moving the pens away from the phone even though I tell you not to touch them! Oh no, oh no, oh no, he's turning purple!"

Tim: "What's going on in here? What's all the noise?"

Me: "He's choking!"

Tim: "Just turn him upside down and hit his back, like this . . . see? He coughed it up. He's fine."

In contrast, our post-Katrina high-stress situations usually go something like this:

Elaina: "Mom, Dane's choking!'

Me: "What do you mean, choking? Can this wait till *Project Runway* is over?"

Elaina: "But he's purple! A jawbreaker is stuck in his windpipe!"

Me: "Hang on. *Okay?* The commercial break's in a few minutes . . ."

All joking aside, this trait—this lack of freak-out—may be a problem when a child has a jawbreaker in his windpipe, but for most things it serves me well. Every summer, when the inevitable threat of a storm arrives at our doorstep, the extent of my preparations usually comes down to making this one statement: "If we need to leave here tomorrow, let's not forget to grab the photo albums and the dog on the way out the door."

I have also become brave about taking physical risks since the storm. For my entire life, outings that involved dark, meandering, alligator-infested bodies of water had been strictly out of the question. One would think this is not an unusual aversion, but my fellow southerners thought it was strange:

Southern Friend: "Wait, are you seriously telling me you refuse to go tubing because you think a snake might come near you? And do you really think a gator is interested in chomping on your fat behind hanging down through an inner tube?"

Me: "Well, it *could* happen. And what I'm really afraid of is not that a real snake or gator will get me, but that a small stick in the water, one lurking just beneath the surface, will touch my big toe or left thigh and I will be freaked, thinking forever that it was a snake when it wasn't."

So, my anxiety level was so high about things most take for granted that not only was I afraid of the snakes, I was also afraid of the thought of a stick that may be impersonating a snake.

Before Katrina, I had always been addicted to cable television news, and easily affected by the doomsday stories and cautions that we all needed to be aware of. I was engulfed in fears over: avian flu; peanut butter allergies; terrorism; the oil crisis; stock market meltdowns; and fragments of suggestive DNA you could see on motel room bedspreads when they were checked with a blacklight.

I also had had for many years a deep-seated fear of things such as stingrays hiding in wait under cover of a thin layer of gulf sand. And let's not forget the sharks, trolling for humans with their toothy and devious grins, fishing the shallow waters of the Mississippi Sound for a menu item known in the darkest depths as Hors d'Oeuvres à la Homo Sapiens.

My fear of stingrays is not completely without foundation. From childhood, I have a vague memory of being on a beach, probably on a weekend trip from our home in New Orleans to either Gulfport or Biloxi. The water was dark; it was a molasses-like surf, continually colored by the dark silt that pours out of the mouth of the Mississippi River, which is nearby. The water looks icky but is beautiful for the abundance of life that flourishes in its salty opacity. This abundance, and the darkness obscuring it, also make the sound scary as hell to swim in.

So in this blurry memory of childhood, there is some type of function being held with employees of my father's company. Families are clustered in bunches, under umbrellas and in groups in the water. I am about seven or eight years old, or maybe even ten. At some point, there is a ruckus a few yards away. It is such an old remembrance that there is little clear memory of what happened. There was something about a man wearing a swimsuit, hobbling from the surf with a deep red trail of blood left behind him. He had stepped on a stingray. The creature had no doubt been quietly resting, defensively hidden under a protective layer of silt until this big-man foot trounced on him in a disorganized game of Marco Polo, or whatever this guy was up to. I have scattered images of the scene a few minutes later, with people huddled around and trying to hold beach towels to his trickling foot.

Who knows the real truth of this story, since it is so sketchy in recollection. But as I remember it, this man lost his foot to infection. For all we know, in reality he just slapped a Band-Aid on it and went out to a disco that night in some high-heeled leather boots (it was the late seventies, after all). Maybe the seven-year-old in me just assumed the worst because my mother had always said, "Better not step on a stingray, because if you do you will need to have your foot amputated." It was almost as if an encounter with rays at a beach were an inevitability and the resultant disfigurement a foregone conclusion. And when we first skipped up to the water's edge on our visits to the beach (which were few, probably due to the impending danger of rays) she would always shout, from the safety of her beach chair and large sun hat: "Shuffle your feet, kids! Stir up that sand so they will not be surprised and lash out at you!" In my mind, all these years, playing in the surf could only end one way: minus one foot.

I always worried about the possibility of shark attack as well. Once while in college or some time after, some friends and I took a long weekend at a condominium in Florida to basically spend the days out on the beaches and spend the nights playing hours of Pictionary and Trivial Pursuit over glasses of very cheap wine. The water there in Florida was not like that in the Mississippi Sound—in Pensacola, you could see what was around you, could see straight through the emerald-green waves down to your feet in the sand. Whenever we were on the beach, my friend Randy would look out to the horizon or look down into the water at a spot three or four yards away from us, and a look of fright would overcome his face. I would see his expression and go into an instant panic, sure that he had spotted a shark, toothy mouth agape and salivating (now, how would one know for sure if a shark were salivating, anyway? Is a shark capable of salivating? Do they even need saliva? Hmmm . . .):

Me: "What? What do you see?"

Randy: "Uh . . . uh . . . uh . . . I don't know! But we should get outta here, *quick!*"

Me: "*Eek! Run!*"

Randy: "Aw, come on, I'm just kidding. There's nothing there at all, I'm just pulling your leg. I like to see you get worked up like that. You look funny when panicked. Wait, hold on a second, what's *that?*"

Me: "What's *what?*"

Randy: "That dark gray thing, circling around over by your left foot!"

Me: "Ahhhh! *Run!*"

Randy: "Ha, got you again. Just joking. But what the hell is that thing down there three feet to your right, looking up at you?"

And so it went, for the rest of our "relaxing" vacation.

And once, when Tim and I had just married and still liked to do things like touch each other while we wore swimsuits, we *were* chased around in the Florida surf by a baby shark. Tim spied it first, and, unlike the faux denizens spotted by Randy years previous, this shark was for real. I screeched and screamed and tried to make it to shore—the thing was *after me*. No matter where I moved to get away from it, it mirrored the movement by quickly repositioning itself within reach of my thigh. It was aggressive and had an interest in me. I saw its face, looked into its cold eyes. Did it matter that this thing was nine inches long and its mouth was the size of a newborn infant's? *It was a shark!* Somehow, I lived to tell the tale.

But something about Katrina did away with much of this fearfulness. Something had made me immune to the idea of sticks posing as snakes and sharks and stingrays waiting to infect or amputate some body part. Seeing a snake draped around my husband's shoulders, and witnessing his survival of it, made me brazen. Living with the elements after the storm, and with the possibility of confrontations with armed looters, and with the days of hard labor that I thought only a full-grown man could pull off was empowering.

So I decided this year that it was time to go kayaking.

We decided to take the kids and we divided up, two to a kayak. We launched the large, orange, molded plastic boats on a muddy embankment of the Okatoma River, a meandering thing that is our version of "moving water." In southern Mississippi, "moving water" basically meant "alligators create ripples in the water now and again when they snack on kayakers too incompetent to keep their boats upright." It is a swift current, almost fast enough to keep mosquitoes and gnats from laying their eggs in it, but not quite. It is so rapid that at times, you are almost unable to see your reflection in it. It is so rapid that if you drop a feather or a homemade origami boat into it, it just may move on the surface if you blow it really hard.

And here we were, navigating the legendary Deep South white waters that I had previously only heard tell of. It was actually happening! I was rowing, despite the pain that crept into my breast and arms after hours at the helm. And we swam in the "rapids" and I jumped from a rope swing positioned on a high embankment, tied probably fifteen or twenty feet from the water's surface. And I went under into the muddy river without a thought, even letting that dark water seep into my ears, knowing full well that I would probably have an ear infection to contend with because of it. But to hell with it—I wanted to *live!* I was living on the edge! I was hanging from a rope! I shared a bath with turtles! I swam in the rapids with gators! I was in a sea of snakes! I was in a sea of sticks that looked like snakes!

Such acts of daring may seem simple to you, but when you have spent twenty years of your life fearfully saying *No!* to expeditions of inner tubing down a lonely moss-draped river with a six-pack dangling behind in the water, you have missed out on more than some mosquito bites and a band of sunburn across the bridge of your nose. You have missed out on: life.

So, in this moment of reflection, a moment that for me is uncharacteristically somber, you learn today of how that ugly, mustached, testosterone fueled and probably syphilitic bitch named Katrina snatched some of our memories, but at the same time freed me up from the fear of making new ones.

I often think now: *what's there to lose?* Why not go *all out?* Here's the thing: I do not stress over feet on the sofa. A few dirty shoes on the sofa, even a few hundred dirty shoes on the sofa dripping in wet tar and dog crap, seem like a party when compared to waterlog. Go ahead, kids: jump. I leave the door open sometimes, letting the air conditioning suck out, wasted, funneled out into the atmosphere like nickels and dimes cast into a stupid, unresponsive wishing well. At least we have walls now. They hold most of the cold in.

I do not watch the network news channels anymore. What's a little E. coli in my lettuce when I survived the greatest natural disaster in U.S. history? Now I would wash myself, even my crack and pits, in front of strangers. I have not needed to do this just yet, at least not since the storm, but when the time comes I am ready and will be able to perform under pressure. I ride roller coasters, but only the rickety wooden kind. I just laugh now in the weird, blank faces of baby sharks.

Since Katrina, I have also indulged in: going sailing without wearing a life preserver or even sunscreen; power boating without first checking The Weather Channel; being pulled in an inflatable tube behind a fast-moving boat with no spotter and a driver holding a Milwaukee's Best; snorkeling in a foreign country without bringing my ID or medical insurance card; jumping into water that may contain sticks resembling snakes and not thinking twice about it; and (once or twice) eating at an all-you-can-eat buffet without using hand sanitizer after touching the serving spoon handles.

Don't think, though, that I will ever take this penchant for derring-do as far as to jump out of an airplane or bungee from a bridge. I will not get lip injections. Or smoke crack, however much I feel that I want to. It is doubtful there will ever be tattoos. I will never be brazen and try something really stupid, like listening to an entire album by Miley Cyrus, even on a dare. I will never drive a race car.

But this can be said now, for sure: because of Katrina, I'm less afraid. Bring on the salivating fish.

14

Middle-Aged Mano a Mano

"You know you're getting older when you don't care where your wife goes, just so you don't have to go along."
—Jacob Braude

Most people identify the "midlife crisis" as something that predominantly affects males. We see the worlds of film, television, and literature populated with midlife collapses. We see men tossing old friends to get new, more exciting ones. We see them tossing boring and weight-impaired wives for newer and improved models, for trophy girlfriends. We also see them go to the Hair Club for Men.

But my husband is not like that. Not at all. The Hair Club is too expensive; plugs are not free. Rogaine is no panacea. He's not a metrosexual, but gold chains are definitely not his speed.

Fortunately, I serve as trophy enough for him. I am not a trophy like a new girlfriend might be; I am not a golden, reflective Oscar statuette stored in a plexiglass case with uplights. I'm more like that little trophy he got once on the cruise ship for being the first to call out "Bingo!" or like the one he got for winning the high school tennis sectional in 1986. They're stored in that old cardboard box on the floor of our closet. This is the kind of box where someone would hoard old scout badges and curled up, crusty boutonnieres from prom night. It is not where you put something you want to impress someone with, but where you stash the things you'd never part with, even if your life depended on it.

The fact that he's recently bought a teensy, weensy sports car means nothing, really.

I know what you are thinking. You are concerned and want to have a few words with me. If you did, here is how our conversation would go:

You: "Wait a second, what are you saying? Are you really trying to tell me that your forty-something-year-old husband has bought a sports car?"

Me: "Uh, yeah, he did, last year. It's a Mazda Miata. I could have lived without it, seeing as cars with only two seats are not practical for family life. But it's the cutest little thing, and it corners well, and it *does* come equipped with a good airbag system."

You: "Yeah, but aren't you worried about this? Isn't a man getting a convertible when he's in his forties almost a joke? Isn't that a cliché of what a man does when he is in the middle of a midlife crisis?"

Me: "Nah, I don't think he's having a midlife crisis. That's *my* territory. He's just finally got enough money to buy things like that, so wants to treat himself."

You: "Well, are there any other unusual signs? Anything going on strange with his cell phone usage, or his job, or his . . . pants?"

Me: "Well, there is this one thing about his job . . ."

You: "Yeah? Go ahead, tell me . . ."

Me: "Well, he wants to quit his job and not work anymore."

You: "You mean not work, *ever*?"

Me: "Yeah. Wait, hold on . . . do you think that's a problem?"

You: "Well, I dunno, depends on what color the convertible is."

Me: "It's red."

You: "Then it's a problem."

And when you think these things of my dearest husband, you may be onto something.

I have asked him about this, about why he feels the need for an excess such as a convertible, when we are both nonmaterialistic and have never really wanted for such possessions:

Me: "Hey, what is all this convertible stuff supposed to be about? Some kind of midlife crisis or something?"

Tim: "What the heck are you talking about? You sound crazy."

Me: "Crazy? Maybe you're the crazy one. Do you think it makes you feel younger or something to have that thing?"

Tim: "No, stuff that makes a guy feel younger is . . . I dunno . . . maybe getting all pumped up and being able to walk around in public with no shirt on. Or joining a rock band and getting a bunch of young girls screaming for you. Or making a touchdown, or hitting a home run. A car does not make you feel young, it's just transportation."

Me: "What kind of transportation is a tiny car that only carries two people? There's no way for our whole family to ever go anywhere in that car!"

Tim: "That's kind of the point of why I bought it."

Me: "Listen to what you just said. This is some kind of midlife crisis. I think you're kidding yourself."

Tim: "Who do you think you are, telling me this stuff? You sit around all day and surf the Internet and wear all that stupid eyeliner that makes you look like a crazy person. You have your . . . things . . . can't I have *mine*?

Me: "Well, my 'things' are free, and yours cost many thousands of dollars."

Tim: "Look, I made the money, I will spend it."

Me: "But if you decide to stop working, who's gonna make money in the future?"

Tim: "I thought that maybe you would. You can work while I drive around in my Miata. And I'll have some extra time, so maybe I'll look into that rock band thing."

Me: "What do you mean, 'rock band thing'? Is a band gonna be one of your other 'things'? Isn't a ukulele-harp gothic pop-rock trio good enough for you?"

Tim: "Look, it's just that I will need something to do when you're working and writing that book of yours. What the hell is that thing supposed to be about, anyway?"

And so it goes.

There used to be a time when our "things" were more of a shared nature. One of our "things" when we first married, and when we only had one small child sleeping in the backseat, was going on "donut drives." Tim had acquired this practice from a friend in college and we later adopted it as a special habit for ourselves. We would just drive around on Sunday mornings in our beat-up old car. We did this while everyone else was still in church, lifting their palms to face upward, offering praise.

We would instead praise the countryside. We lifted our palms to the acres and acres of longleaf pines and live oaks that are everywhere down here, or to the marshy areas filled with swamp grasses and what is surely the best bowfishing in the world. We would make fun of people's homes, picking out the ones we would live in and the ones we would refuse even if given to us for free. We ducked into old service stations that were somehow still operating, and found their mini-marts always had freshly picked green peanuts by the pound and some kind of pickled eggs, floating in sour red juice. We tried to find nooks and crannies of roadside we had never seen. We would eat donuts from a mixed box of a dozen until we almost felt sick, and finally head home when low blood sugar made us want to doze.

In recent years, the donut drives have dwindled. Instead, these have been our two biggest "things": the kids.

When kids come along, the average couple is typically thrust headlong into proper care and feeding. At least in the early years, these budding little people are hobbies par excellence. They leave little time for diversions. But now that ours have both entered the world of T-for-teen video games and *Lord of the Rings* books and standardized tests, they are not as interested in us as they once were. They will happily spend hours staring at electronic screens and pressing little buttons on controllers until fingers are sore and eyes are permanently fixed in a trance. They will watch DVDs without the aid of a parent to explain the finer points of the plot. And at least the oldest one, our son, has reached the point where he really and truly thinks we are dorks.

Tim and I now have more time for our own *individual* "things." And sometimes, as is often the case with people our age and older, his "things" are not necessarily mine. And this is fine. I would be highly surprised if he enjoyed pasting fake eyelashes to his lids, or listening to hours of music from the 1980s while surfing the net looking for people to talk with about how to craft effectively with plastic sequins.

But there are times when our midlife crises clash. His needs for novelty and free reign clash with mine, and we're in a death match. We become like Bobby Fischer and Boris Spassky. Their game was chess; ours is crisis management. Each player stares across at the other, trying to figure out what the next move will be, trying to figure out what can be slipped by without notice. We battle mano a mano for the freedom to re-craft ourselves into wiser, braver versions of the people that we used to be. We battle to see who can act like the bigger fool.

I fight to return to my self of the summer of 1982, the one who roller skated and wore cherry lip gloss. Tim grasps for the remains of that little kid who played cops and robbers and learned the church organ during the

Carter years. And we both fight tooth and nail on behalf of our untapped selves, the ones who have yet to be imagined, who lie in wait, barely embryonic.

But between us, this simultaneous reaching forward and backward began to, at times, be a balancing act; it began to involve weird contortions of which our middle-aged minds are increasingly incapable.

Tim: "Okay, it's Saturday. How do you want to spend your day?"

Me: "You are so nice to ask. Let me see . . ."

Tim: "Don't get carried away, now. I was asking 'cause I'm going driving around, maybe stopping at the music store to get some good Aerosmith sheet music. Then I thought I'd hang out in Barnes and Noble for a while so I can research what else I'm gonna do when I stop working forever."

Me: "*What?* I thought you were asking so we could do something as a family, or at least so I could go somewhere by myself while you watch the kids."

Tim: "I work all week and have no free time. You don't work right now and have all the free time in the world. You will watch the kids while I have my day."

Me: "But today I was going to go stand in line for concert tickets. It has to be done today, they go on sale this morning, and it'll sell out in just a few hours, for sure. And getting them online never works so well. I can't take the kids! They will drive me crazy. When they get bored they do stuff like pulling on the wires to my earbuds, as if they want me to stop listening to music and pay attention to them or something. It's so *annoying*."

Tim: "Well, looks like we have a conundrum here."

Me: "How about we just solve this by us both staying home? We can do some family things and interact with each other with some low-grade resentment as we always do."

Tim: "Okay, I guess that's the only solution."

So we do this, and are surprised every time how much fun we have, despite the low-grade resentment. We enjoy "Thing 1" and "Thing 2." We have fun when we play Uno cards and Scrabble and Clue, and when we go on walks in the neighborhood, and when we take them to a swimming pool. They both smile, happy that mom and dad are taking a few moments away from their respective crises to pay some attention. They remember how it used to be when they were littler and more dependent, and they feel nostalgic. My daughter becomes a blooming flower; my son does not think we are dorks, at least for the afternoon.

And in these moments I may think for a bit of my own selfishness as of late. I think how much it must hurt my kids. I recall the almost daily moments when I had been too self-absorbed to have the time to notice the events of their lives, too distracted to cheer much for the lost tooth or lament the badness of the schoolyard bullies or the time to just . . . be with them, doing nothing. But when I get to thinking about this, I mean *really* thinking about this and feeling guilty, it always ends with me saying: screw 'em.

I have enough foresight to know the truth: some day they will get even. Some day—and some day soon, in the case of my son—they will hurt me, too, when they drive off to their first date, or to college, or to that big new out-of-state job. And I remember that all of these things, these moments spent together, these driving aways, and these moments of selfishness, are all simply parts of a life cycle.

Tim and I are at the dawn of an interesting part of that cycle. According to experts, the average midlife crisis lasts anywhere from two to five years in women, and from five to ten years in men. That is good news; it means that mine should be finished before long. It means, according to experts, soon I will gladly go back to wearing Mom Jeans without embarrassment and making to-do lists of things that actually might get accomplished. They tell me that soon, perhaps within a year or two, I may even go back to my natural hair color.

This is good news. It means there will be a few more good years with my kids once this blasted weird psychology wraps itself up and fizzles out. There will hopefully be a few years to hear about how some jerk gave them a wedgie at recess, or how they got to read their most outstanding essay in front of the class, or how they don't understand the freaking word problems. Those years will give me a chance to build more memories with them before the inevitable day I am carting their laptops and blue jeans and mini-fridges away to some state college or other.

Once I am done with my second childhood, I will attend to their first. I will keep them busy while my husband finishes his job of becoming a rock star using an Aerosmith songbook. I am hoping that the five- to ten-year period of the male midlife crisis looks more like five years and less like ten, but I am prepared for the worst. I am prepared to stare this thing down. I am prepared for a constant checkmate . . . for keeping his wily king always on the run . . . for watching my own back.

Luckily, there is one thing on my side that may help. Without a job (unless he happens to go on a massive world tour with his band, or something along those lines), my husband will no doubt have a difficult time paying for any more Mazda Miatas. And in a few years, something important will happen, something that will change all our lives for the better and perhaps pull him from the open road. It is something that will bring him back to us . . .

. . . he will be screwed by the warranty.

15

The Future Mrs. Two Cakes

"The really frightening thing about middle age is that you know you'll grow out of it!"
—Doris Day

It is difficult to have balanced instincts about work.

If there were tiny aluminum Monopoly pieces that best represented the extremes, one would show a thirty-year-old businessman in his coffin, wearing an expensive suit. The other would be of a very skinny homeless guy, a starving artist, with holes in his shoes and fingers lost to frostbite. In the game of work, it's difficult to know which piece to choose; both lead to a different form of loss. Without my husband's generous gift of fifteen years of get-out-of-jail-free cards, I would have been forced to choose one of these fates.

Since I started writing again about six years ago—working for a while as a staff reporter in a newsroom and as a freelance journalist for various magazines and websites—I've apply myself in ways most definitely out of balance with my earnings. There'd be no way to measure how much I earn per hour—I'm quite sure that toothless meth addicts working at quickie marts make roughly the same hourly wage. The income of mediocre pole dancers is probably similar to mine, but only if you double mine and then multiply it by a factor of ten.

The publications I work for are always happy with my work. What they don't know, however, is I'm not at all devoted to them; I'm simply devoted to the words they ask me to write.

In contrast, when young, I was entirely too committed to whichever company I worked for. I soared as a devoted model of efficiency and customer service. The sale was always rung up correctly, or the right pair of jeans was handed over the dressing room door at precisely the right moment. There were sometimes customer comment cards taped to the walls of these workplaces, saying "Kara helped me so much!" Or, "What a great representative!" In college, I worked energetically on campus and overseas organizing study abroad opportunities for students. As an adult, I worked assiduously before I was married and for a few years after, in sales. I worked hard, even after giving two weeks' notice. I spent what felt like eternities sitting in Dilbert-esque cubicles, talking on the phone, staring at a computer screen, and typing till I had cricks in my neck.

But the worst pains back then were the unacknowledged cricks in the mind.

It is easy to cast your nose always to the grindstone, trudging away as a blind cog in some capitalist venture or other. But at some point, in our darkest moments, while eating from a tub of ice cream at night, or while sitting on a beach on one of our ten yearly vacation days, our instincts might say that this kind of productivity is really a crock. We know in the most secret and protected parts of our soul that when we were children, we didn't dream of spending our years giving sales pitches or entering data. We dreamed of becoming bohemian artists, or world-famous baseball stars, or photographers who snapped images of every nook and cranny of the Sahara and every mystical temple in Bangkok, and then developed them on Kodachrome. We dreamed of being authors and of dancing beautiful dances and of claiming patents that would save the world.

I understand that some of you workhorse types would consider this negative and regretful attitude one of a quintessential Generation X slacker. And by most standards, you'd be correct. But damn straight if I don't wonder now how I could ever have cared whether I met a quota or came up with a decent proposal or represented some company or other professionally at a trade show. Now I care about representing only one thing: me.

Granted, there is the need to make money. We all need money. We want to afford the finer things in life, such as maraschino cherries and brand-name dryer sheets. But pretending to enjoy the process of representing stuff that isn't "Me"? That, I can no longer understand.

I know what you're thinking. You're thinking, "How ungrateful can you be? You sat back for fifteen years and let your husband support you while dog hair tumbleweeds blew through the foyer and avian flu marched forward somewhere in Asia."

You think, "You say these things while all across America, people are being laid off from their crappy cubicle jobs and wish it weren't happening."

And you would be right in all of this. But these uncomfortable facts do not make me want to take up a "real" job. Not as a profession, at least.

When young, I never imagined I'd ever be on the husband dole for as long as I actually was. I had always worked, from before it was legally permissible for me to do so. And I had worked *hard*, sometimes taking as many as three part-time jobs simultaneously. I loved money, but more important, I loved the pride of earning it.

But now, I'm thinking all that early minimum wage careerism caused a type of burnout. I was like a fast-burning flame of youthful earning power that peaked early and now has turned completely cold. That is all a poetic way of saying: damn, I've gotten lazy. Not about my writing work, but about the idea of "The Man."

My first job came at the highly illegal age of thirteen. Who knows how the donut shop managed this, or why my parents permitted it. But I'll be damned if I didn't learn a lot about the world by hanging around cops and street punks and real-life characters a young teen seldom gets to know while walking in the mall or skateboarding around a cul-de-sac. This particular place seemed more neighborhood bar than coffee shop. It was always packed with regulars. It was smoke filled and diverse and filled with people who liked to hang out at all hours. It was a place where question-able deals often went down on the payphone, and where you could easily find the working-class underbelly of the New Orleans suburbs. It was very adult; it was a venue that I at first felt frightened in but later felt inured to.

The real world and I met there at age thirteen. I learned quickly what a pair of eyes looks like when their owner is either drunk or high on some really primo pot. I learned how to work not for the shop but for the tip jar. I learned to steer clear of certain people, peculiar men with sloppy fat rolls about the waist and graying temples. Those guys are old men now, but even back then I knew what they were thinking when they would watch me a little too closely from behind their coffee mugs and cherry turnovers.

Often I played the role of the bartender. Patrons vented to me, told tall tales, and had violent, sometimes physical arguments while standing in front of our shelves of French crullers and deep-fried apple fritters. Sometimes they would hand each other little rolls of money, or argue, or shout obscenities at each other in a characteristically New Orleans accent. Sometimes they would behave like this with a little powdered sugar from a donut on their upper lips, or scattered randomly in their mustaches, and it would make the spectacle that much better. These incidents convinced me growing older was often a complicated, and sometimes bitter, thing. That was the takeaway message at age thirteen. I didn't want to grow up to be like them, gray templed and unhappy, ruts of worry on the brow, arguing in front of a case of jelly donuts.

There was hour upon hour to study these elders in a setting where they had no interest in appearing as anything other than what they were. I saw how set in their ways some of them were.

There was one quiet man in his late forties or early fifties that I called Mr. Two Cakes. He came in at precisely the same time every Sunday afternoon. He always ordered two cake donuts and a cup of coffee. *Every time* he ordered exactly the same thing. Rain or shine, winter or summer, it was two cake donuts and a cup of coffee. He would eat them quickly and look at the counter or the sugar shaker or the ashtray while he ate. What's more, he always came alone and *always* left behind an uneaten donut half and a fifty-cent tip.

This man was like clockwork. After several months, I began to fill his inevitable order as soon as his midsize sedan drove into the parking lot outside. Sometimes I had the urge to scream, "*Please*, for God's sake, invite someone to sit here with you one day!" I swore I would never get like Mr. Two Cakes, would never become so old in mind-set that I wanted things to always be exactly the same. Every Sunday, I would think, "Go crazy, Mr. Two Cakes! Order hot chocolate and an éclair, and eat the *whole damn thing*!" But of course, I never said anything at all for going on six years of serving him virtually every Sunday afternoon. I never even said, "Coffee refill?" or anything daring like that, because it was clear he'd just wave me away. Once I considered giving him a donut and a half, just to see what he would do, but was not brave enough to upset the subtle equilibrium.

In addition to Mr. Two Cakes, I vividly remember the thirty-and-forty-something ladies who worked the night shift. They were rough-looking single moms who were struggling to keep their kids out of central lockup and keep sneakers on their growing feet. They had sad wrinkled faces and cigarette-stained fingernails, and made me apprehensive about the prospect of becoming the age that they were then. They never seemed to look forward to anything, or have enthusiasm for anything but their next smoke. When they worked, the registers often came up short. As I recall, a few bucks and some loose change occasionally disappeared into the shadows of the night, no doubt to buy sneakers and cigs.

There were legions of police officers in the shop, since they always ate for free. The police were always the best tippers, especially during Christmas, when they would pin dollar bills to the small holiday tree that stood behind the counter. They would plaster the tip tree with George Washington. I really liked the police and their Georges.

What was less likable was the fact that they always had looks of resignation concerning their jobs and the prospects of apprehending criminals. Sometimes I'd overhear a frustrated person—sitting there having a warm glazed donut and cup of hot chocolate—tell one of these officers about some crime or another perpetrated on them:

Donut Patron: "And you would not believe, they even tried to take my Betamax machine. But they didn't get away with it. They dropped it in the yard before they cleared the fence. So at least I got that back. And thank goodness my *Ghostbusters* tape was still inside, unharmed."

Officer: "Well, thank God for that! They were probably gonna sell *Ghostbusters* for drug money."

Donut Patron: "That's what I was thinking! Is there something else I oughta do to help catch the guy?"

Officer: "Well, did you file a report?'

Donut Patron: "I did."

Officer: "Were there serial numbers on any of the items they took?"

Donut Patron: "Yes, a few of them!"

Officer: "Were there any cars in the area?"

Donut Patron: "The neighbor wrote down the license plate of a suspicious car that was idling in front of my house on the night and time of the break-in!"

Officer: "And did you have any kinda security system on the premises?"

Donut Patron: "Yes, I even have a video surveillance system with a video that shows the asshole breaking in."

Officer: "Can you see the guy's face clearly?"

Donut Patron: "Yeah, clear as day!"

Officer: "Oh, well good for you!"

Donut Patron: "So, how long do you think it will take for them to catch 'em?"

Officer: "*Catch him?* Nobody's gonna catch him."

These wonderful officers of the law were just like everyone else, midlife guys who were trying to make sense of things, who were lonely for their kids who had grown up and left the nest, and lonely for their own youthful days back when they took their oaths to the force and to the wife, believing in both wholeheartedly. Now they just rode the same streets year after year and pushed pencils around in a coffee shop, filling out forms. They still hoped that somewhere in the mix, some good would get done.

So, just before my so-called midlife crisis started, I had begun to realize I had indeed become like these patrons of the coffee shop. A homemaker with nowhere to really go each morning, I had begun to wear the same clothes day after day, eat the same things day after day, and harbor the same fears and phobias, day after day, year after year. It had become normal to watch the same things on TV, talk to the same people. I'd been putting the same pink slippers at the foot of the bed each night before climbing in. I had put them on in the same exact way every morning, loving their familiar molding to my feet. Left foot first. Right foot, shoved in quickly, at an angle. Every morning I had brushed the same, washed the same, used the same coffee cup with that colorful cat picture on it that had been my favorite for years. And I don't even like cats.

A routine attitude toward living established itself over the years, and it wasn't at all unlike that of those donut shop cops. When I thought of the young and exuberant me, the one with all the dreams, the photojournalist and world traveler and music critic and high-fashion model (okay, I just added that last one for the hell of it), I would think: *Catch her? Nobody's gonna catch her.*

So, in the interest of changing the routine, an obvious, and quite responsible, thought occurred: I should get a job. *Any* job. Something crazy, like being a prison warden or a mortician. That would, indeed, force me to do some things differently. It would shake things up a bit.

I would wake and have no reason to crawl back into the warm bed after putting my kids on the bus. Thought would actually have to be applied to what I wore. I would choose a different shoe every morning, on purpose. I would sometimes put them on right-foot-first, sometimes left, sometimes while sitting on a toilet or while surfing the net before work. When I drove to my job, I would play something new on the radio. One day it would be some fearmongering on NPR about global warming. One day it would be something weird to do with Psalms. One day it would be a morning-drive guy ranting and raving about "homos" and the cost of gasoline. But it would always be something.

When I got there I hoped I would see different faces. Some of them would be genial, some of them pissed, and I would talk to those faces next to some kind of water cooler. They would tell me about caesarian sections and box seats and work reviews. I would hear tales of success and of desperation. It would be even better than cable TV, particularly on Fridays.

I eventually took a staff job with the news—where I got some of these things—but only stayed a few years and I eventually went back to working for them freelance. So . . . I am still stuck in the working-in-my-slippers rut . . . and who wants *that*?

Truth be told, I'm glad I've done what I always wanted to do—writing—but it's not enough. I need to shake it up more creatively, which is why I have written this book you are reading now. The clock is ticking down to the day when I will be seen as a *Mrs.* Two Cakes in the eyes of some kid working at a Starbucks. Only now they probably call those types Mrs. Two Lattes or Mrs. Two Mocha Frappuccinos.

Speaking of, maybe I should ditch this book writing stuff and get a job at Starbucks. That would be a nice change of pace, although it's doubtful it would be anything like the donut shop. It is doubtful I'd be lucky enough that anyone there would be seriously high at noon, or in debt to bookies, or cursing at each other with powdered sugar stuck in their goatees.

16

The Principle of It

"Middle age is that perplexing time of life when we hear two voices calling us, one saying 'Why Not?' and the other saying 'Why Bother?'"
—Sydney J. Harris

I was embarrassed by my parents while growing up. I'm not speaking here of the everyday kind of embarrassment, the kind that comes from being seen in public with a parent who wears high-water pants or too-tight leisure suits. I am speaking about the kind of shame that makes you want to run away and join the circus, or storm out one night after an argument over homework and spend the rest of your days as a streetwalker, or an accountant, or some such horror. It's the kind of embarrassment that makes you wish you never had parents at all.

When they would publicly direct some form of discipline at us, or at a stranger, it was the worst. Take, for instance, our trips to the local supermarket. If cans of peas and corn that should have rung up for twenty-nine cents register instead as thirty-nine cents, a ten-minute episode of public embarrassment would begin. The manager would be there, proudly displaying his name badge and an expression of authority, the "Store Manager Game Face." You could always tell he knew my parents would be a real headache. The cashier would be there still, standing by with her supermarket apron, picking debris from under her nails. She never cared enough to look ashamed of the error. My mother and father would wait there in a militaristic stance, sometimes for as long as fifteen minutes, to collect back the shiny dime they were due. My sisters and I, we would fidget around with the Milky Ways. My father would say, "Don't touch that!" or "Act right till we get this fixed!" or some such thing. I found out at a fairly young age that unless the thing is chock full with toilet paper rolls, it is generally futile to hide behind a grocery cart to avoid embarrassment. The world of people who do not collect misappropriated dimes can still see you crouching there, behind the shiny metal grid.

As a kid, it made no sense. Why do this? Why go through all this for such a token? Why make your family want to crawl under a rock, or go hide outside in the scorching heat in that hatchback Datsun we used as a family car? Why make the customers in line behind you want to bludgeon you with the frozen pot roasts that had begun defrosting in their carts? Well, we all know the answer to those questions: *It's the principle of it.*

> principle of it (noun): The mistaken notion that an error can somehow be cosmically corrected by expending even more time and energy than had been caused by the error itself. As in "If the electric company cannot get this bill right, then we won't use electricity anymore. That'll show 'em! It's the principle of it."

As we age, slowly, little by little, we begin to understand the *"principle of it"* principle. We begin to notice in our timeworn psyches an ever-growing expectation that there'll be something called: justice. Our maturity also tells us this may be a pipe dream, this justice business. We know that some things just are not fair and that the world has always been in a state of unbalance. We persist nonetheless. We begin, roundabouts the age of thirty-eight or forty, to see the virtues of going without electricity in January just to make a point.

It's an unusual feature of middle age that one begins to lose embarrassment over things. We will point out mistakes and think nothing of it. We will ask for refunds. We will demand service. We will tell people who are behind us kicking our seat in the theater or on the plane that they damn well better stop. Sometimes, we will even say: "Please, *please*, can you shut that baby up?" We will walk around with toilet paper stuck to the bottoms of our shoes. We will complain to waiters when there is a fly in the soup, or when they seem to have some kind of attitude. More commonly, we will engage in rutabaga showdowns.

Surely you have been in rutabaga showdowns, so you know exactly what I am talking about. I found myself in one such showdown earlier this year:

Me: "Um, excuse me, but those rutabagas were supposed to be on sale and my receipt doesn't reflect the sale price."

Clueless Supermarket Cashier: "Your *what* is supposed to be on sale?"

Me: "Uh, my rutabagas."

Clueless Supermarket Cashier: "Ruta-*what*?"

Me: "Rutabagas. Turnip-like root vegetables commonly found in soups and stews. Botanical name of *Brassica napobrassica*."

Clueless Supermarket Cashier: "What??"

Me: "It's that big softball-shaped thing you rang up for $2.50 a pound when you should have rung it up for $1.43 a pound."

Clueless Supermarket Cashier: "Oh. Well I can't fix that. You need to go to customer service to get that one fixed."

Me: "You mean that place over there, which has about twenty people standing in line? Are you saying that because of *your* error, I need to spend half an hour standing in line?"

Clueless Supermarket Cashier: "Look, lady, I can't do nothin' 'bout it."

Me: "You *could* do *something*! You could ring up the goddamned rutabaga *correctly* from the *beginning*!"

Clueless Supermarket Cashier: "How you 'spect me to ring it up right when I don't know what it is? Next time just don't buy weird-ass vegetables."

Sometimes, when you are a woman in the middle of a midlife crisis, you will find yourself actually putting in your two-cents worth with the U.S. Postal Service. One would think years of experience would have taught against such ill-fated campaigns . . . but no such luck. You do it for a reason stronger than the dictates of logic. You do it for "The Principle of It."

Me: "Hey, I was just wondering—why do you guys close this post office for an hour every day?"

Clueless Postal Worker: "Oh, that's our lunch break."

Me: "But there are two of you working. Doesn't it make more sense in terms of customer service to stagger the lunch breaks so at least one window can remain open?"

Clueless Postal Worker: "But then people would complain that only one window is open, so we just close it all down."

Me: "Are you kidding? You seriously think its better for the taxpayers who use this post office to find a locked door at noon every day instead of finding one open window where they can mail their packages and buy stamps?"

Clueless Postal Worker: "Basically, yes. We don't want to hear about it, so we just shut down and go to lunch."

Me: "But it's ten days before Christmas! I am a taxpayer! When I come here *ten days before Christmas*, I expect two windows open, or, at the very least, one window open! Consider the needs of the people you serve. Some of them take off work specifically to come here and mail their grandma's Christmas present, and find *no open windows*! Some people throw away a whole lunch hour of their own just to drive here, only to find a locked door! This is an outrage!"

Clueless Postal Worker: "Lady, what do you *want* from me?"

Me: "A book of stamps, the kind with the nutcrackers on them. If not, the ones that say 'Love' will be fine."

Sometimes, as was just illustrated, there isn't a point in pursuing "The Principle of It." Not because we have done the generous thing and exercised some forgiveness, but because we recognize the futility.

But when I was younger, I was willing to forgive. It never seemed futile back then. And you really do need to be willing to forgive in order to dance the bump with a Nazi.

I had this experience long ago, of doing the bump with a Nazi. You know how it is. You're in a disco, and there's a Nazi there, getting down to some Donna Summer under a disco ball. Just a normal night out on the town.

It's 1990 or so, in Austria. Apparently, Donna Summer is still popular when the locals are not engaged in chopping wood for the winter or in doing the chicken dance. He's not some sleazy bar guy you met but an old man, a renowned author and former colonel who had previously been instrumental in commanding parts of Hitler's army, instrumental in strategizing the most effective ways to kick some American ass. He had led men to take sniper shots, to lob grenades, to blow off arms and legs, to unknowingly implant PTSD, to organize attacks that may have killed your neighbor's grandpawpaw. He had made bad stuff happen.

Maybe I'm being unfair. Maybe he technically wasn't a Nazi at all, and was just a brilliant career colonel unfortunately tasked with helping Hitler defeat us. But as far as I'm concerned, anyone pointing and directing on or around the beaches of Normandy, wearing a big ole Iron Cross and those oh-so-stylish but darkly corrupt clothes, was on the Nazi-fied side of history. I'm not going to be a stickler for details.

This old colonel is now well-respected, acknowledges the evil of the regime he once aided, and is a special guest of your employer. You are given the unspoken task of being nice, of holding no grudges, of feeling that well, yeah, we all have skeletons in the closet. Forget that some might have *actual* skeletons in there, hiding with the overcoats and galoshes.

So this colonel is "reformed." Because of his confessions and regrets—and understanding that basically *all* German and Austrian young men were in the army back then—he apparently is now respected both at home and abroad. He now tells lamentable and cautionary tales in classrooms and auditoriums. He explains what it was like to work under a regime characterized by great taste in clothes and hairdos but a horrific lack of morality. He is also as cute as hell, gray haired, well postured, fit from a lifetime of climbing alpine rock faces and cross-country skiing to the supermarket. His khaki pants have crisp front pleats. He speaks a heavily accented English and is probably eighty years old, best guess.

You are twenty and are forgiving, so you do the bump. There is no "Principle of It" yet. Without Donna Summer there to help, maybe that former Nazi would have been left standing on the dance floor alone, swaying those arthritic Aryan hips to the beats and wails of a beautiful black woman all by himself. But when we are twenty, that does not happen. We forgive. We touch our hips to old Nazi hips. We touch our hips to any hip. We just dance. Especially to Donna Summer.

When we are in our forties, not so much. One would think that perhaps a midlife crisis *would* make you want to cut a rug with an aged and repentant person who had tried to take over our country. There seems to be a certain appeal to it, a certain shock value, a certain feel to it that resembles giving the middle finger to anything that is too serious.

But when you are actually tumbling face forward down the other side of the hill, the last thing you want to do is make excuses for anyone anymore. Maybe it's the act of realizing, finally, that there are no more excuses for your own angry disposition, or for your own lapses in judgment, or for the blubber around your thighs, that makes you unbending. You realize everyone is also culpable for their own dispositions, lapses, and thunder thighs. Unlike when you're young, you increasingly feel—when you get to a certain age—that we all make our own hells, our own heavens. We might feel that the bum is at least partly responsible for his dirty shoeless feet, and the ghetto kid for his drug habit, and the annoying mother-in-law for her tiresome persistence that you are not good enough for her son. We feel that Congress is at fault for its own debacle. We feel that our parents are no longer to blame.

It rarely crosses your mind at all that even a Nazi can have a midlife crisis. It never occurs to you that maybe his crisis entailed a look back and a thought: "What was I doing all those years? Why was I trying to help take over the world? Maybe it's time to change course. I think I'll take up gardening." When you are somewhere post-forty, you usually have a hard time forgiving the mistakes of youth when those mistakes partially involve genocide. Genocide is not at all like smoking a doob on the way to class, or getting in a fenderbender, or "doing it" in some bathroom, unprotected.

Hard and unforgiving or not, I would probably now be unyielding if I met this old man. You've gotta admit, it's one thing to look at the first half of your life and say, "Geez, I didn't accomplish what I set out to do. I always wanted to scuba dive, and I still have not done it." But it's another thing entirely to look back on that first half and say, "Geez, I didn't accomplish what I set out to do—destroy America on the beaches of Normandy."

So, I would like to say that my midlife crisis does know some boundaries. *It's the principle of it.* I can honestly say that a line can now be drawn at dancing with former Nazi colonels, however sweet and repentant they may be. If I could go back in time to that night in the disco, I would not dance. I would have had a single drink of American-made Jack Daniels, despite the fact that it tastes nasty and makes me do that shiver. I would have tipped my glass to people who had the foresight not to lob rockets for dictators in their youth. I would have tipped my glass to an entire ethnic group—one with a rich and beautiful culture—destroyed. I would have tipped my glass to your neighbor's dead serviceman grandpawpaw.

Now, if I get an offer to jitterbug with Caligula, or do the twist with Napoleon Bonaparte and his fabulously big ego, or square-dance with Ghengis Khan, I cannot wholeheartedly swear that I would say no. But a reformed Nazi colonel? That's where I draw the line. I'm too much of a patriot. *It's the principle of it.*

17

Midlife Ripe

"What a strange illusion it is to suppose that beauty is goodness."
—Leo Tolstoy

Sometimes, a woman's body is described as "apple" shaped if she holds most of her excess weight around the mid-section. She is "pear" shaped if she carries this weight almost as fleshy saddlebags on her hips, thighs, and backside.

I'm a pear. Have always been, even before puberty saw fit to give me any definition of silhouette or cravings for heavy cream. But it must be admitted, however, that I take deep exception to these terms of "apple" and "pear." No offense intended to my friends of the gay community, but: I ain't no fruit! And I especially ain't a fruit that is always either so hard you can't eat it or so ripe that it is mottled with bruises.

Just like avocados, pears always mean trouble. Something is so momentary and unpredictable about the pear and the short delectability timeframe it affords us. There is a very small window of opportunity for the pear to present as the optimum in deliciousness. It will just sit there hard as a rock for a long-ass time, tart enough to pucker your lips if you were dumb enough to bite into it prematurely. Then it ripens perfectly, in a blink. If not seized during that fleeting moment of perfection, it is tossed, gooey and brownish, into the trash bin with the used coffee filters and junk mail.

But back to the subject of our bodies: honestly, this fruit nomenclature is just downright ugly. I think I hate it. It isn't appropriate at all to describe our rear ends and abdomens and shoulders in such terms. Shouldn't we always describe our bodies as the beautiful things that they are, useful for their work as the greatest tools of our lives, instead of as sweet little juicy tidbits? Shouldn't we always praise, always herald, our fatty, organic selves as the best of biological chariots, taking us up mountains, or into swamps, or to do some lame Tae Bo, or on a pompous march down some aisle?

Surely some old man of a doctor came up with this apple and pear crap. He probably had a few scraggly eyebrow hairs that were too long. I bet he oogled his test subjects in the laboratory when he did the BMI calculations and fat-people-underwater floats. I propose that we reject his stupid fruit analogy and instead adopt something that celebrates the beauty of our female form, such as my name of choice for the pear-shaped woman: "An Egg on Two Toothpicks."

This is how I have always envisioned my figure, as an egg, set upright with the widest part at the bottom, supported with two peg legs. This always seems to be the general shape of my silhouette, especially when wearing a skirt. I have seen photos of myself, even while still in elementary school, where you could see a big full skirt, rounded over a rump the size of Everest, thighs beneath like the Himalayan foothills, and tapering under the skirt into two skinny little legs that look like nude-colored air strips leading up to base camp. *An egg, on two toothpicks.*

Now I don't know in the foggiest what to call you apple gals—you are on your own in that department. You might as well go ahead and start your own club, get your own secret handshake. It's not as if it would really be a secret anyway. We can all see who you are. We see that you are the ones who can sit in airline seats without worrying that your hips will touch the person sitting next to you. We can see who you are, but we Eggs on Two Toothpicks don't give a hoot. The plight of the slim hipped is something I do not understand at all. May as well keep calling yourselves "apples." See if I care.

So anyway, one day many years ago I got it into the ole noggin that I wanted to lose weight and shape up. So I dragged this rotund egg with side saddlebags (need to hold the Twix bars somewhere!) off the sofa, tentatively stood up on the points of my wooden picks, and took one small step toward my somewhat lofty goal of looking like Angelina Jolie: I joined a gym.

Not only did I join a gym, but I also met with a personal trainer. We met on the smelly wicker couches at the front of the club. They were the kind you always see in Florida condos, with removable cushions showing birds-of-paradise. I don't now remember this guy's name, but rest assured he was fit and good looking. He was somewhat along the lines of Tom Cruise, only sane. And here is what happened at our first meeting:

Sane Tom Cruise Trainer: "So, Kara, what exactly do you want to accomplish over the next six weeks?"

Me: "Ha, that's a funny question. What do you think I want to accomplish?"

Sane Tom Cruise Trainer: "Well, I don't know. I'm not a mind reader. All I can do is take a look at you and surmise. But I don't want to do that."

Me: "No, that's okay. You *should*. I'd actually *like* you to take a look at me and surmise."

Sane Tom Cruise Trainer: "Well, from what I can see, what we have here is—"

Me: "Wait, hold on. We're sitting down. Don't you want me to stand up or something? How can you tell what my problem areas are when I am sitting? What about all that apple and pear stuff?"

Sane Tom Cruise Trainer: "Oh, don't worry. *I saw all that I need to see.* I'm a guy. It only takes a second."

Me: "Oh, it does? Only a second, yet you still didn't want to 'surmise'?"

Sane Tom Cruise Trainer: "I just don't want to make any assumptions, you know what they say about assumptions, they make an ass out of—"

Me: "Yes, yes, I know about assumptions. But you still felt that you had enough information within the first few minutes of seeing me—"

Sane Tom Cruise Trainer: "First few seconds."

Me: "Right. First few seconds. And I guess you gleaned in that blink of an eye that I look like an egg balanced on two toothpicks?"

Sane Tom Cruise Trainer: "Sure. Doesn't take a brain surgeon. Classic pear."

Me: "So what do I do now?"

Sane Tom Cruise Trainer: "Well, we get you on a nice five-day-a-week aerobic workout routine, perhaps start slow with the treadmill and then work up—"

Me: "Okay, I can handle that—"

Sane Tom Cruise Trainer: "At the same time, we get you on some weight-lifting, but only for the upper body."

Me: "Why only upper body?"

Sane Tom Cruise Trainer: "Well, with so much . . . hip, and quite a large surface area of . . . rear, it would be better to not bulk it up and make it all appear *even larger.*"

Me: "Oh, is that right?"

Sane Tom Cruise Trainer: "Yep. You want to build some serious muscle in the upper body, which will act as a balance to the *bulk* you have in that . . . hip area. You can do some isolated calf raises to help pump up your calves if you don't like that toothpick leg look, but that's up to you."

Me: "Oh, is it now? Up to me?"

Sane Tom Cruise Trainer: "Yes. But it's not as difficult as it seems. I mean, people come in here thinking they will have great bodies when they are done, but sometimes this can't happen. What you need to hope for is health, and we can work together to use what you've got to your advantage."

Me: "What have I got?"

Sane Tom Cruise Trainer: "Your collarbone is well defined, which will make you *appear* slim, at least when you are sitting at a table. Your lower arms and wrists are okay. We just need to beef them up and get some meat on the shoulders to widen your look. To create diversion . . . to create . . . illusion."

Me: "To create . . . *what*?"

Sane Tom Cruise Trainer: "Illusion. We make the upper body look bigger so the hip area seems like it's actually in proportion."

Me: "Well, if you're gonna create an illusion that makes *this* look sexy, then you damn well better hope you're as good as David Copperfield!"

I was angry. He didn't take kindly to my comment, or to its obvious lack of enthusiasm for his plan. Maybe it is because I had played the David Copperfield trump card. He knew in the depths of his heart that this body reshaping business was a load of crap, and that his phony gym-based illusions could not even hope to match up to the spectacles crafted by one of the world's most popular and tantalizingly cheesy magicians, David Copperfield. He saw the hopelessness of it all. I mean, surely he knew that making only the bottom half of an egg disappear may be even more difficult than making an entire car disappear from behind a curtain with the wave of a hand and the blink of an eye? And, could it be that he was, perhaps, just a wee bit jealous of David Copperfield? Seriously, back then that dude had a formidable head of hair on him. And sexy assistants.

So now, whenever I set out to lose a pound or two, I remember the advice this "trainer" gave me. Sometimes, he had attempted to say, change *could* happen by way of a series of illusions, by way of some small sleight of hand. You could work and work and work and never achieve your goal. You could pound on a treadmill every morning, next to that guy watching the stock ticker on the TV playing CNN. You could climb the StairMaster. You could finally get that metabolism completely under control. You could pump iron with a tight belt cinching your waist and make those funny faces while you do it. You could glance around to see if anyone is noticing all of your effort. You could pump the biceps in the mirror and pretend you are just checking your form. You could do all of that, and erroneously think you will lose the weight in the places where you want to instead of in your left elbow and in the crook of that bunioned toe. After all that, at your age, you could still have nothing to show for it, or little to show for it. But if you have the right Tom Cruise Trainer, you sure as hell could take the easy way out. You could craft an illusion of . . . *something* . . . in a short time frame.

I wonder sometimes if this philosophy could possibly apply to other areas of my life. I wonder if any amount of illusion crafting could somehow take away or mitigate a little bit of the downsides of midlife. I wonder if it could take away the crow's-feet that are gaining ground; or end the struggle for a new identity now that the children require less of me; or just dissipate the simple, everyday blahs. I wonder if it could mask the boredom, or beef up the obituary, or lubricate the joints. I wonder if some illusion or other could take away the feeling of being suspended between two poles of life, in a no-man's land: not quite rotten, but not at all unripe.

Oh my God, just as I am writing this, I realize something important beyond belief! This *is* my moment! *I am ripe!* I'm not a tart young hard-body whose season is still unfinished. Neither am I the stuff of compost, the rotting detritus that failed to become someone's dessert. I'm just a woman.

Here is what I am: I am between two poles. One pole is old and diapered and has yellow toenails. The other pole likes to chew gum. But I am only now, at this very second, realizing that I am not suspended in a limbo but am floating in a kind of glory.

Maybe midlife isn't a curse after all. Maybe I have seen this all wrong, and it will turn out to be an absolute gift, a snapshot in time that I didn't see for what it was. It seems so clear: at this very moment, and *only* at this moment, I can choose which way I want to lean. Let's just hope the toothpicks can hold me up through these leanings, these swayings back and lurches ahead.

Let's celebrate *now*, at least for the fifteen or twenty minutes while I am still believing this all to be true. Let's celebrate a moment I will never, ever have again. I will never be *exactly* this again: middling. I can fudge to one side and seem a youth. I can careen a tiny bit upward, and I am wise. It feels somewhat like freedom.

I am, simply, ripe! Tell the men for me; tell the coffee klatches; shout it from the rooftops, scream it into the mic at the next PTA meeting. Do it quickly! To hell with David Copperfield and fitness illusionists who resemble demented Scientologists. When you are ripe, at that one and only moment in time, you need no illusions. You need no smoke, no mirrors. You just: *are*.

I am so glad I realized this today. Seems it's not so bad being a midlife pear, not so bad at all, at least at this very minute. It seems there will never again be a better time than this to hug the saddlebags, or to rise up on those toothpicks in defiance, or to imbibe in an obvious sweetness.

18

Ten-Point Cabbage

"At middle age the soul should be opening up like a rose, not closing up like a cabbage."
—John Andrew Holmes

Around here, we are fond of parades. They are not the kind of parades you are probably familiar with, where crowned beauty queens ride on the backs of fire trucks. They are the kind where people hand Jello shots down off decorated floats to complete strangers and where a bearing of breasts to strangers is quite ordinary.

You see, around here we have Mardi Gras.

Mardi Gras is the festival celebrated on Fat Tuesday, the last day before the Catholic period of repentance known as Lent. This pre-Lenten bacchanalia is a time to let loose before those dark weeks of abstinence. And if New Orleanians are going to have to spend six weeks in prayer and repentance, six weeks in fish sandwiches and evening mass and acts of penance large and small, they feel they damn well better have memories of boobs and Jägermeister shots to pull them through. So this is a *religious* festival, which the tourists find hard to believe.

The carnival season consists of several weeks of private parties, parades, and Mardi Gras balls, where the grand old families of the city dress as they have for over 150 years, as kings and queens. The kings are usually elderly. They often look to be on their last leg, waiting to be usurped by a challenger, or waiting for their final leech treatments before succumbing to "bad vapors." Obviously, it takes a number of years to amass enough social prestige to rise this high in the ranks. They always have on faux powdered wigs and powerless but impressive scepters superglued with Swarovski crystals. They drink in goblets.

The queens wear enormous gowns, products of months and months of expensive design work. Their bodices and long trains will be like artworks.

They will often feature birds, or gardenias, or elegantly posed shrimp, satin and sequin tributes to that particular year's theme. The most elite of queens, such as the Queen of Rex, will have on nothing but gold, and crystal beads hanging from her frame like mini-chandeliers. There are elaborate head-pieces similar to those worn in Rio de Janeiro. Most of the time the head-pieces are so large that they cannot actually be worn without the aid of ropes and pulleys and scaffolds. When they parade, two small pageboys in Buster Brown wigs and saggy tights will bring the queen drinks and hand-fuls of beads while she is attached to the scaffold and pulleys and hooks. I would love to see, just once, the point at which the expensive champagne has made its way through their systems and these queens have to use the smelly, underclass Port-O-Let hidden in the bowels of the float. I think of that every year, of the irony, and of the royal stress. I think of the pageboys holding the door shut and hoping the float does not suddenly stop, sending the crown jewels into a lurch. They will say: "Your majesty, are you done yet?"

Attendees at the balls, where such queens and kings are announced and celebrated, wear black tie and tails. They bow to these nobles as if they were actual royalty instead of what they are, which is rich people in costumes.

What they are actually bowing to is the fact that these faux royals were lucky enough to be born with a certain last name. Even though I was born and bred in the city, most of my family comes from an hour southwest of town. I bear a common Cajun maiden name: Martinez. It is not pronounced as you have usually heard it, but as it would be said by a French peasant after drinking too much cooking sherry: Martin-ez, with the stress on the "ez". Not so long ago my people crawled out of the swamps of Lafourche Parish speaking the French of Acadia. As children, my grandparents only spoke French and had to be taught English in school. My ancestors were trappers and fishers and hunters. They raised chickens and stalked game and sold meat and animal pelts and weird halfway-to-voodoo herbs. They were Catholics. They would have had no reason for a Swarovski scepter, except perhaps for the fact that it may make a shimmery catfish lure. My ancestors never rode in coaches or carried brass-tipped walking canes and copies of Victor Hugo novels.

Neither this local name, nor my German married name, has any reso-nance at all with the society people of New Orleans. If our family tried to become a member of one of these elite carnival krewes, here is how the application process would go:

117

Buffy: "We have here someone wanting to join our ranks named Bachman. Do you know any Bachmans?"

Muffy: "No, I have never met anyone from that family. That's not even a French name. Who do these Bachmans think they are?"

Buffy: "I know! Maybe he works over in the oncology department, or maybe it's one of those nouveau-riche families that think they can edge in here and put on gold lamé costumes with us. *As if* they are entitled to wear gold lamé with a name like Bachman!"

Although we would be rejected from the more society-oriented activities revolving around Mardi Gras, we gladly partake in festivities designed to entertain Plebeians. Our carnival parades involve costumed float riders tossing plastic beads and trinkets to the huddled masses below. The riders will slowly pass in these very elaborate and beautifully decorated papier-mâché floats. On the floats will be nods to the past, usually. There will be themes celebrating the stories of Homer, or of some god or another, or of philosophers and thinkers. There will be tributes to exotic nations and times, to long-gone places like Siam and Persia. Mostly the themes will all be very old world, a celebration of the favorite ideas of the elite, a poking fun at what has been taught in their expensive boys' prep schools over the years. And there is the irony that this is all played out on a modern tableau, where drunk people wear flashing neon necklaces while standing next to a distorted paper and glue depiction of "Leda and the Swan."

There are also the delightful parades that wildly skewer or rebel against these old traditions. They are equally fun and never fail to please with their huge colored paper bosoms and Kermit the Frogs and Zulu kings wearing coffee cans for crowns.

All krewes toss these garish strings of beads recognized the world over as being from Mardi Gras. They will toss plastic cups for us to pour our drinks into while we watch them frolic in their gold lamé. They will toss stuffed plush toys to the children (my children have actually caught board games and backpacks at Mardi Gras parades). They will send sailing over the crowd, and usually into the hands of the most attractive among us, garter belts and tiny see-through underwear that bear the name of that particular krewe (usually Greek or Roman names such as Endymion or Bacchus or Hermes). The protocol is that this underwear should be worn over a pair of blue jeans if you are a girl and over the head if you are a guy. I have seen newborn infants wearing G-strings in this way, their little fuzz of peach hair fitting right into the crotch. It is only in New Orleans that you will ever see a four-month-old with a lacy thong on his head that is screen printed with the words "Happy Mardi Gras. Heads or Tails?"

Good thing for us, Mardi Gras does not happen only during these days preceding Lent. A lot of tourists do not know or understand this. Mardi Gras happens for us all year, as it is not an event but a way of life; it is a *philosophy*. Around here the ethic of carnival seeps into every celebration, infiltrating like a weird communicable disease. At Easter, there are parades celebrating—guess what—the *end* of Lent. There are midsummer parades to celebrate the fact that Mardi Gras is thankfully only a half-year away. There are Christmas parades where riders recycle their leftover Mardi Gras–themed throws from the year before. Nobody cares if they catch trinkets saying "Happy Mardi Gras" a week before Christmas. Hell, who cares about Christmas, anyway? We have Mardi Gras.

But our favorite off-season (it's funny how around here we call the rest of the year "off-season") parades are the St. Patrick's and the Irish-Italian. We have attended these for many years. These two favorites roll down the streets of Metairie, a suburb adjacent to the city known for its exemplary big-box stores and strip malls. But on these days—days such as Fat Tuesday or the weekend of the Irish-Italian—it becomes like a fantastic playground. Families line the long parade route, waiting all day at the same street corners they had occupied on every year of their lives for this same event. They eat spicy fried chicken, or open bags of peanuts, or feast on potato chips that make them endlessly thirsty for sugary drinks. They toss footballs and the kids whine "But mom, when will it *get* here?" The grandmas sit back on old quilts to enjoy the favorable weather. And it does not get better than this.

There are few tourists; this event is all ours. The weather is always beautiful, the kind of days we rarely get in the Deep South, days that are breezy with a vibrant and color-saturating sunlight. We always know that springtime is about to deliver itself up to the grips of summer scorch, so we appreciate these last days of reprieve. There are marching clubs, where the men in the colors of Italy or Ireland travel on foot, trading roses for kisses. The papier-mâché floats left over from Mardi Gras are repurposed for the day's theme—an Elvis float becomes "Elvis Goes to Ireland" or a float showcasing a twenty-foot-tall Batman becomes "Is Batman an Irishman?"

And here is the delightful part. No doubt there are other cities where you can get your hands on a nice, smelly head of cabbage at some St. Patty's celebration or other. But this is something altogether different. This is something that can feed your family for a year.

In addition to the plastics, the Irish and the Italians love to throw us food. They toss not only cabbage, but also potatoes, carrots, bananas, apples, citrus, garlic, and the items that are my favorite for their rarity: bars of Irish Spring soap, pasta, and ramen noodles. The ramen must be part of a Chinese-Irish contingent, because it makes no sense. It seems like some-body is breaking a rule with that one.

Speaking of rules, if you have never been to a parade down here, you may not know the etiquette of all this. Believe it or not, there *are* rules. In fact, there are so many that a book could be written on them. For instance, if something lands on the ground, say, a shiny bauble or a bamboo tribes-man's spear, and you are able to place your foot atop it, it is yours. If two people grab a pair of beads at once, it should be relinquished if the other person is either very young or very old. Another rule: if you catch some-thing that looks like a plastic penis hanging on beads, be sure to hang it around your child's neck. I have never enacted this unusual rule, but it seems to be presently on the books because I have observed it time and again.

There is also a protocol regarding the catching of throws. You must ask for what you want. Be specific if you want a metal doubloon or a stuffed animal shaped like SpongeBob SquarePants. You must always yell thank you. Remember, these people are throwing you their aging produce and plastic injection molded stuff out of the goodness of their hearts. They spend hundreds or thousands of dollars on things that you would kill someone for at the moment, but then bring home and throw into the garbage. This is because you know it is only about the competition. It is survival of the fittest.

To win the competition, you need to make yourself seen. You will fail if you just stand there and randomly wave an arm around. You need to *work it*. That means catching the eye of a float rider and not letting up on them:

Plebeian: "Hey, you with the red hair, throw me something! A pair of long beads!"

Muffy: "Only if you take off your shirt!"

Plebeian: "I can't, my wife and kids are here!"

Muffy: "Well, do *something*!"

Plebeian: "Okay, I'll do the Robot!"

Or, you can resort to my husband's technique, a surefire winner that he used when our children were babies:

Tim: "Gimme some carrots! Food for the baby! He's starving and needs to eat!"

After hours of making eye contact and doing the Robot or whatever, we trudge home from one of the best days we'd had all year and throw it all away.

When I was younger, I did not see the sense in what some parade-goers would do for the Irish and Italians. They would arrive with plastic buckets and, sometimes, handcarts and large garbage cans on wheels. They did this because they had an interest in catching a metric ton of cabbage.

I used to think: a head or two of cabbage and a few carrots—that sounds about right. I could toss 'em in a pot with that corned beef that is always on sale around that time of year. That way we could participate in that widely practiced mystical tradition of hoping for a bit of good luck via a smelly pile of cruciferous vegetables.

But as time passes, as the approach of middle age makes me not care how foolish I look while doing the Robot, I see the virtue of getting while the getting is good. I want as much cabbage as I can get. I fancy the notion of filling up our freezer with the generous donations of rich people. I like the idea of reaching into there, on some boring evening when nothing at all is happening, and feeling jovial for a second when I grab ahold of a Ziploc full of spoils. Those bags of freezer-burned produce bring me back to the days of sitting in our folding chairs, of watching the kids draw borderline perverted things with chalk in the street while waiting for the first float. In this way, the cabbage *does* bring good luck. In addition, it is nice to have so many vegetables in the house that I never need to fight over the price of rutabagas.

I have started to love this competition. The past few years we have shown up at the parade with a red wagon and pile of contractor-size garbage bags for holding the booty. I wake up early on those mornings. I fret about the weather. I attach a feathered 1970s-style roach clip to my hair, a sort of lazy costume. I get out my dusty hiking boots with the steel toes—this is *serious business*. We always play New Orleans music on the way. We would never play that Irish stuff, because as far as I am concerned, this is still carnival. We listen to songs about kings and queens, and sexy local women, and getting drunk, and clichés about gumbo, and street gangs squaring off while comparing costumes. We listen to a music of absolute joy.

Five or six hours later when it is done and we are tired, we push an old baby carriage filled with cabbages and new potatoes back to the car. We take photos of every year's take and compare them to see which year we did best. We really do this, I swear that this is true. If I could show you these pictures I would, especially the one where I was pregnant and had hormonal skin discolorations that appeared on film as a complete mustache. I am standing there above a formica counter full of stuff, arms spread in a presentation, as if on *The Price Is Right*. My faux-mustache makes me look like a French chef, or a little like one of my Cajun ancestors. I am like a weird vegetarian huntswoman, posing with a pile of produce instead of a ten-point buck.

The drawback to all of this is that I spend two days standing in a hot kitchen, chopping and blanching and freezing cabbage and carrots in quart-size bags. I do appreciate how little value these items have, but still have enough responsibility about me to try to make use of the spoils of war.

I am a Cajun, and I so dearly want to pretend I'm not hunting for sport.

19

Ground-Floor Life

"Probably the happiest period in life most frequently is in middle age, when the eager passions of youth are cooled, and the infirmities of age not yet begun; as we see that the shadows, which are at morning and evening so large, almost entirely disappear at midday."
—Thomas Arnold

Some time during the George Bush Sr. presidency, around 1990 or so, there was a rally held outside One Shell Square, the Shell Oil building in downtown New Orleans. A few hundred people, mostly young, gathered together in a concerted effort to prevent the deaths of American soldiers that were sure to arise as a result of the Gulf War.

They wore those gray brimmed caps that made themselves look like commies. They had on block-printed skirts from the Andes, and T-shirts with all-organic tie dye, and chandelier earrings, and those loose cotton smocks with ties at the neck that are imported from Kathmandu. They had hair that was orange-red from henna washes, or had traditional and purposeful afros, or, for the white guys around age nineteen, had statement-making dreadlocks. These guys had hair uncombed and matted down from months of neglect, hitting their shoulders in long chubby locks that looked like something you would use to scrub your sink, or rough up some wood. There were also many Earth Mothers, women inspired by a reverence for stuff like dung and seed pods and the sky.

They wanted to play the bongo drums and sing Bob Dylan tunes, although Dylan had not really been heard on New Orleans radio for many years. But more important, it can be imagined they simply wanted to get in on this prime protest opportunity:

Protester Dreadlock: "Yeah, man, my uncle was at Woodstock. I missed out on that. Damn, I wish there were still a Vietnam around so we could protest it."

Protester No-Bra: "I get you, I do. But I do feel this is a ground-floor opportunity. We're getting in here early, so we can say we were there first. There was Stonewall, there was Selma, and now there will be the march on Shell Oil. I'm telling you, this is ground floor."

Protester Dreadlock: "I dig that. It is ground floor. Now we just have to get some good chants going. Can't shape world events without a few good chants."

Protester No-Bra: "Yeah, I get ya. I've been working on this one. How does it sound? 'No blood for oil! No blood for oil!'"

Protester Dreadlock: "Sounds pretty good, I dig the blood imagery. And I like the talk of oil. But what does that have to do with invading Iraq?"

Protester No-Bra: "Well, you know the filthy capitalists are always grabbing at oil and we don't want them to. So why send in people to die for it?"

Protester Dreadlock: "Wait, hold on. I know this is ground-floor shit and all, but I don't know if I could support it. I would personally die for some nice organically grown safflower, wouldn't you?"

Protester No-Bra: "Wait, dude, is that the kind of oil they're dying for?"

Protester Dreadlock: "Look, all we need to do is know that it's wrong. And to bang our drums. And to march around wearing John Lennon–style sunglasses. Leave all the minor, unimportant details to the Democratic Party guys."

Now, at this point a Democrat reading these words may be thinking, "What the heck is this that I am reading, a Rush Limbaugh book?" Or he may be thinking, perhaps, "This is exaggerated. Nobody is like this!"

But I swear to you, people *are* like this.

I know this because I was there that day, at the great historical march on One Shell Square. I carried some silly sign and envied those who were enterprising enough to bring their own bongos. There had been meetings on my college campus over the course of previous weeks, discussing important issues such as the virtue of having a few dozen bagels available the morning of the march, and what color Sharpies we should all use to mark up the free-speech poster boards.

On the day of the march we walked in circles for hours around the building, stomping in no uniform fashion on the white stone slabs surrounding the base of the sleek high-rise. No doubt Shell employees on coffee breaks must have glanced down from their office windows. They likely looked down at our collective action while blowing into their steaming mugs to cool the morning beverages. We wondered, "How, oh how, could they not be stirred by our passion?"

We sang. We bongoed. Some organizers shouted carefully crafted slogans into megaphones. We chanted, sometimes apparently about salad oil. We ate bagels. And then the United States of America entered the small nation of Kuwait, liberating it from Iraqi tyranny. The war was won in just a handful of days. The war was short, but it was: ground floor.

It has been many years since that less than fateful day, and I saw fit to move on to other things. But I still liked things to be somewhat "ground floor." When I moved away from home and got that first apartment, I was a little disappointed it was not on the ground floor. It was hard to navigate a shared stairwell in the dark on a Saturday at 2:30 a.m. after a night of indulgence. And years later when on vacation, I was always angry when we needed to lug baby carriers and strollers up hotel stairs. Why were we never on the ground floor? The front-desk workers would say, in their typical East Asian accents, "Well, that discount coupon is only good for third-floor rooms." So we always had third-floor rooms. As if the indignity of hearing the next-room-over sessions of coitus and yelling that are always present in places with paper-thin walls were not enough.

And then, a few years ago, we considered a new kind of ground-floor opportunity:

Tim: "I want to move away from here, to somewhere new."

Me: "Why?"

Tim: "I'm sick of always having to work so hard. Guess I just got worn out after Katrina and the fatigue of the storm has never gone away. I work day in and day out, then I come home and there's some work to do with the house, or with the kids. I feel like my life is an uphill climb."

Me: "You feel that way because we have a two-story house. You are climbing steps every day. That's why it seems like it's all uphill. Maybe we do need to move. Maybe it's time for something more . . . I don't know . . . ground floor."

So what was once a brotherhood of ground-floor safflower users hoping to move mountains had, a few years ago, dwindled in number to become nothing more than a lone almost-middle-aged couple, staid by life, but still somehow hoping to stage a great Anti-Stair-Step protest. Such are the philosophical and social changes that often accompany growing up.

Winston Churchill obviously knew that the way we look at the world tends to change, as we often age in ways that are quite predictable. He is credited with a quote that I used to scoff at but now understand:

If you're not a liberal at twenty you have no heart; if you're not a conservative by forty, you have no brain.

Now of course Churchill makes a huge generalization, but it does seem if there is a flow to this evolution of thought and heart as we grow to adulthood, it is that it more often than not flows in the direction he describes. It flows toward the curmudgeonly. It flows toward the sane.

Who knows how or why such radical change comes along for many of us. Perhaps the seeds of change are planted when we look at that first real paycheck:

Me: "Hey, look! My first real paycheck from a full-time corporate job! Let me take a look here . . . okay, they minused off something here for health care, guess I gotta have that . . . life insurance . . . I have no kids or anything—do I really need that? They could probably pay for a funeral by selling my old Eurythmics VHS tapes and Rick Springfield posters—they would really bring in some serious buck."

Roommate: "Nah, you're right, you don't need that life insurance stuff."

Me: "So I should get rid of that? Yeah, I could use the $4.62 each month to buy something else. And what else is here? Well, there's Social Security, they took something out there . . . and the 401(k), I guess I should do that . . . but wait, here's something big—what is this withholding crap all about?"

Roommate: "I don't know, I think that's just taxes."

Me: "Taxes? I thought you have to pay those in April."

Roommate: "Yes, I think you are paying them early."

Me: "But wait a second—is the pothole out there in front of our house that keeps screwing up my alignment getting fixed early?"

Roommate: "Uh . . . I dunno. I think it's for more than potholes. It may be for welfare or something."

Me: "Well, it better not be for half-a-baguette foundations! I know what that's about and I can't support it! If you can pay to get to Europe you can afford to buy your own friggin' baguette!"

Roommate: "I don't have any clue what you are talking about."

Me: "Well, I'm definitely cutting out the life insurance. I'll save that and put it to something useful."

Roommate: "Maybe when the lease expires we can put it toward a better apartment on the ground floor."

And so it probably goes in second- and third- and fourth-floor studio apartments across the United States: life insurances are canceled; paradigms are shifted; curmudgeons are born.

One aspect of being interested in such things as paycheck withholdings, ideas and how they shape public policy, the ramifications of political battles and elections, and other such subjects is that there is an entire industry devoted to feeding this hobby. There is, as you read this very book, a huge flock of unattractive people in Washington, D.C., and elsewhere who rely upon their analytical acumen and Harvard educations to tell us, in breaking news segments, which politicians are sleeping with someone other than their wives. They also tell us exactly where, on what street corner and in what dark alleyway, the squandering of the public trust is happening. They give details of the dresses worn by people at $5,000-a-plate luncheons. They tell us who to vote for. They tell us, in riotous and angry directives, who not to vote for if we don't want America to go to hell in a handbasket. There are pundits and talking heads and reporters and gossip columnists. There are twenty-four-hour cable television channels devoted entirely to educating us on these critical need-to-know items.

I had barely noticed that twenty-four-hour, around-the-clock "Breaking News!" had become the soundtrack to our family life. While we ate dinner we heard of political backstabbing and baby stroller recalls. We heard of promising cancer breakthroughs and of how Mel Gibson went off on some rant. When we sat on the floor and played board games, like Candyland, or Chutes and Ladders, we listened to talking heads talk about other talking heads. They often gave opinions on someone else's opinions. When we helped with the homework, we did it to the background drone of news broadcasts; our lives had become a symphony, conducted by mass media outlets and with the accompaniment of Shepard Smith or Anderson Cooper or George Stephanopoulos. It was no way to live.

But it had been clear to me, always had been, that politics and news are for the college-educated what NASCAR is for everyone else (whether they live in Alabama or not). Real politics is a somewhat high-minded entertainment that, in its best form, is really only for the intelligentsia. It is for the denizens of think tanks and for smart glad-handing types. It is also for their television-watching groupies, the ones who all wish that they, themselves, had gone on to grad school.

In reality, politics is sport. It is competition. It is diversion. It is a reality TV program par excellence that *mostly* reflects some kind of . . . reality. But the part of my brain that knew how the television skews the real world was in denial:

Me: "But we *need* to know what is going on at every minute! We *need* to know what that other candidate is up to! We need to know what bills have passed! And we *need* to know what George Will has to say about it all!"

What made this news habit worse were the attacks of September 11. What had previously been a need to be in the know suddenly became an obsessive interest in hearing every tidbit, however small, of breaking news. I could not miss the finer points of any given public policy debate; I could not miss a moment of analysis by those I respected, or by those I hated; I could not miss a single . . . high-speed police car chase. (See what I mean? NASCAR.)

But there was something about that day several years ago—that day when my youngest child got on the school bus for the first time—that I finally realized: *watching the news sucks.* Perhaps, just perhaps, I didn't need to watch it anymore. *Maybe I could be free.* Maybe I could go out and stir things up for myself. Hold my own rally. Run for my own political office. Start my own nonprofit. Make some cardboard signs. Stage my own high-speed police chase, talking on a cell phone the whole time and driving erratically through Los Angeles, tipsy.

So I stopped the news, cold turkey. Ripped the satellite television wire out of the wall. Dismantled the receiver box. Lobbed it forcefully in the trash can. Realized: "Damn, now we can't watch VH1 anymore—*why didn't I think of that?*"

But the decision was fruitful. Instead of watching a half-reality orchestrated by newscasters and fellow journalists and copywriters, I started to pay attention to my own reality, to crafting it. Sometimes, crashing it into walls, losing tires, going up in flames. At other times, careening along at high speed. But one thing was for sure: I was in the driver's seat.

So *take that*, George Stephanopoulos and George Will and Anderson Cooper. I had no problem saying good-bye, even to you, Anderson, who is so adorable. I had no withdrawal symptoms. I had no cravings. I had no DTs. I didn't even miss that breaking news ticker that runs along the bottom of the screen. You are all lovely people, but I no longer care a whit what you have to say. I no longer care that the ice caps are melting or that some president's wife likes an ornament on a tree. I no longer care what is in the new budget, or what color is favored this season in Milan.

I *do* care again, however, about "ground-floor" opportunities, kind of like I used to. But for some reason this time they are not political. I care about ground-floor great music; ground-floor moments of gossiping with my daughter about cute boys; ground-floor Halloween costume buying; ground-floor snuggling with my husband on a Sunday morning; ground-floor dog petting; ground-floor laughter; ground-floor damn good shrimp fettuccini. I care about getting in on the ground floor on a great deal, a deal that has more to do with writing poems sometimes when there is nothing pressing to do, and with making fun of my friends, and with looking at old photo albums from when I was three. I care about getting in on something ground floor. I care about ground floor . . . *life.*

What the heck. I'm so motivated now that I think I'll stage a protest. I'll gather up a raving throng, from somewhere in my living room. We will make signs and buy some bagels and give the kids bottles of bubbles with funny shaped wands and put radical tie-dyed flowers in their hair. We will have no need to talk into a horn or mic. We are loud. We are angry, and dammit, we're not taking it anymore!

The protest needs to be about something important, something as earth-shaking as safflower oil. It will need to be about an issue that *really matters.* It will need to be about something befitting the interests of a mom, of a suburban housewife, and of a member of the human race.

I think we will protest dreadlocks.

20

The Good Fortune of Cosmetic Damages

"The harvest of age is the recollection and abundance of blessing previously secured."
—Marcus Cicero

Many years ago, before moving into the home we owned on the Mississippi Gulf Coast, we spent a great deal of time exploring with real-estate agents. We nodded our heads politely about "open, airy" homes on golf courses; we halfheartedly considered fixer-uppers with old brown shag carpet, scant wafts of mildew in the air, and virtually nonexistent mortgages; we traipsed into myriad identical tract homes of new construct, careful not to stray from the butcher paper rolled out over the new carpet or hardwood floors to protect them from our apathetic shoe-sole markings.

One morning, we received a call from a new agent about a house she said we just "had to see." It was priced significantly below appraisal, was in a nice location, and, because it was in foreclosure, was being let go for a song.

The house seemed, from the street, a behemoth of a thing. It was pinkish bricked, with a steep, pointy roof and white trim and large arched windows. With expectations high, Tim and I waited on the sidewalk out front while the agent fumbled with long fingernails to get the key from the lockbox attached to the door.

It was funny to watch her. She seemed like something out of one of those old beach party movies my mother loved to watch. You know what I am talking about—the ones that starred Annette Funicello and those peppy sorts. In those films they would all go to clambakes and wax surfboards and make out in little grottoes in the rocks and sing songs on the beach with pointy, swimsuited breasts that looked like torpedoes. They wore one-piece suits and high heels and had on very pale nail polish and lipstick and a pretend girlishness and had all sorts of womanly curves.

This real estate agent seemed like them, and was *outdated*. And when you hear a critique such as this coming from someone like myself, who still would actually wear a pair of early '80s parachute pants if they made them in a large-enough size, you know you can basically trust it. If she seemed a little behind the times even to me, then it must have been true.

She seemed like somebody who would serve you "sweet tea with a sprig of mint." Kind of a southern beach party Stepford Wife, if you ask me. She was miniskirted. She smiled real hard through capped teeth and had a singsong smarmy voice and a very large brownish bouffant coiffure, reminiscent of a beauty queen, circa 1960-something. She finally got the door opened.

Big-Haired Agent: "Now. Listen, y'all. I know this house needs a little sprucin' up. But it's only two years old, so all the repairs will be just for surface cosmetics. Believe me, what's in the walls is sound . . . its all up to code, is energy efficient and virtually new."

Me: "It looks unkempt in here . . . um . . . it almost looks . . . how do I say this . . . trashed!"

Big-Haired Agent: "Well, that's why it's such a beauty of a deal. Seriously, all y'all need to do is get a cleanin' crew in here for a few hours and you have a new home."

Me: "But there are dirt and food smudges on literally every surface in this house. I can see that it would be light and airy if it weren't bogged down in filth!"

Tim: "Yeah, look here—there's a huge grape jelly handprint on the mantel . . ."

Me: "And look—there's a peanut butter handprint on the pantry door! We could make a sandwich from the food on the walls. I don't mean to be judgmental, but—"

Big-Haired Agent: "Okay. I sense a problem here. I understand that y'all could make a PB&J with the fingerprints. I get that. But perhaps y'all are not looking at this place the right way. Look at it through the Lord's eyes, not through your own."

Me: "Huh?"

Big-Haired Agent: "If the Lord were looking for a new place to live, he would not judge a home on things like, 'Are there, or are there not, fingerprints on this house?' No, siree. He would say, 'Judge not . . . lest ye be judged.'"

Me: "Um . . . okay . . . but for some weird reason I have a feeling The Lord would not choose a tract home that is in foreclosure. Or that has popcorn texture on the ceilings. He could have anything he wants—He's The Lord!"

Big-Haired Agent: "Listen, y'all. You never can predict his ways. He is a mystery. His ways are known only to himself."

Me: "Would he know why there's a large smiley face painted on the bathroom mirror in red lipstick?"

Big-Haired Agent: "Oh, The Lord would probably agree with me that the person who did the lipstick drawin' was probably just upset about being evicted. Look, it's just lipstick. Like I told you—the problems here are strictly *cosmetic*."

So we do our normal nodding and pretending we will consider the property, knowing full well by now that we'd never buy it. We point out the nice high ceilings and good asking price and say we will think about it. We try to gently rush this grand tour, to move on to the next house. We lightly feign interest in the exterior for a minute or two, to let the agent know we are at least giving full consideration to what she's shown us.

Tim: "Termite tunnels."

He grimaces, pointing down at an earthen pathway made of red dirt. The tubular passageway clings to the house, a termite superhighway that is usually a telltale sign. It leads from the lawn, up the side of the concrete house foundation, and on into a weep hole gap in the bricks, about six inches from the ground.

Big-Haired Agent: "That *may* be somethin', but its probably just some dirt that needs to be hosed away. Y'all could have it looked at by somebody."

She nervously adjusts her bouffant.

Tim: "I *am* somebody. *I* am looking at it. It's a termite tunnel."

Big-Haired Agent: "Look, do y'all pray?"

Me: "Huh? Sorry?"

Big-Haired Agent: "Do y'all pray? To The Lord? I mean, what religion are you?"

What does one say to an agent who believes that God would live in a foreclosed home in South Mississippi with lipstick mirror artwork and termite tunnels that are really just piles of dirt? You say the only thing that makes sense:

Me: "We're Jewish."

And what makes total sense about this response is that we are not at all Jewish. We just wanted the conversation to end.

Big-Haired Agent: "Well, that's just fine . . . that's okay. I have never met one until just now. But I can tell y'all that the Lord will not mind one bit if we join hands and pray over whether he wants y'all to live in this house here."

Tim: "Okay, let's let The Lord put in his two cents."

Big-Haired Agent: "Well come on then, y'all, let's join hands and make a little circle."

She self-consciously examines her own peach-colored fingernails before grabbing my hand, angling them to momentarily catch the glint of the midday sun. She touches her hair again.

We join hands and stare at the ground as the prayer starts. I begin to giggle uncontrollably, picturing us and this strange woman we had just met praying together in the driveway about a dirty tract house. I imagine people turning onto the street and driving by slowly, rubbernecking, thinking we were holding an impromptu tent revival, only without the tent. Snake charming. Or termite charming. I imagine them thinking: "What in tarnation?" and finally deciding on getting out of their cars to join in on the foreclosure praise.

Not wanting to show disrespect, I somehow convert the unstoppable laughter into what appears to be sounds of religious rapture:

Big-Haired Agent: "Oh heavenly Father, this young couple doesn't know whether this home is right for them. You always do well in pairin' people up with the right home."

Me: "Haha . . . I mean, hallelujah!"

Big-Haired Agent: "I'm feelin' this home is right for them, but only you know for sure. So we pray that you'll lead them to the right decision."

Me: "Hehehe . . . he knows the answer!"

Big-Haired Agent: "Amen to that! He knows the answer. Show them the way. Amen."

Tim: "Uh . . . amen."

Big-Haired Agent: "You see, Mrs. Bachman? I knew that would be helpful. He's gonna watch out for y'all. And you were moved by the spirit—are you *sure* you are Jewish?"

I feel quite sure that if there is a Lord, he looked after us that day. He saw fit to not put us in a home with termites and lickable walls. He deserves some credit in this regard.

Sometimes I recall this story when I think about our lives, of how lucky we have been. In middle age, I feel this even more acutely. We have never had a serious illness; we have never had financial woes that keep us awake at all hours of the night; we have never battled addictions, aside from ones that involve Twinkies and disinfectant and Internet forums; our minds are mostly sound; our children sleep safely in their beds and their pediatrician does not even recognize them, because he sees them so rarely. We are, indeed, blessed by good fortune.

Why do we have this fortune? Is it because we spot the termite tunnels of life, and somehow sidestep them? Or, is it because somebody, The Lord, or fate, or Zeus, or just the universe has had our back?

Even though I am staring down the barrel of midlife, I feel gratitude. I feel pretty lucky to be staring down that barrel. I feel appreciative for every day of making fun of people who do not get my jokes, or who have the gall to wear skinny jeans. I am appreciative for being here to wear my own ugly pants; other people need something stupid to laugh at, too. I am glad to be here to mock modern-day Annette Funicellos for your enjoyment. I am glad to be mostly in good working order—glad that my TMJ-plagued jaw occasionally works, that it goes up and down and allows me to say, "What in tarnation!" when I chance upon something interesting in the world. I am glad that my eyes still cry when my best friend calls and cracks me up with a story or two or three. I am glad that cancer hasn't gotten me yet.

The reason this cancer figures into the gratitude equation is that my mother, the one who loved beach party movies, died of it when she was in her early fifties. It was an aggressive cancer. It was already stage four on the day that it was detected, after a few weeks of pain in one hip that she thought was from weight gain, or from sleeping funny. Turns out that it was just one of many tumors. One of a thousand points of light, thousands of monster cells that lit up on her CAT scans and MRIs like evil little constellations in the night sky of her body. A thousand points of: death.

So as my forty-sixth birthday approaches, this thought looms: If I have my mother's genes, I may have eight or so years left. Or six, if we count the date she was *diagnosed* with cancer. Or five, if we count from the date that the first demented and purposeful cell was probably born and metastasized. So sometimes I wake up and think: a few years to go, baby! Better do something with it.

I try to use this insight as more an inspiration than an excuse, but sometimes it's difficult to resist:

Tim: "Um, I know you enjoy your time on Facebook and Twitter, but do you think you could spend a little time washing some dishes, or maybe doing some laundry? I am down to this one pair of drawers, and have worn them for three days already."

Me: "How could you say that to me, knowing my condition?"

Tim: "I didn't know that excess facial hair makes people unable to do dishes."

Me: "No, not *that*, silly. I mean the cancer."

Tim: "The *what*?"

Me: "The cancer. You know what I'm talking about, the cancer that's going to get me in exactly four years, on my fiftieth."

Tim: "That sounds like something crazy—like when you were afraid to go in the water because you did not want to be afraid that a stick may be a snake. Same thing."

Me: "Not at all! They are so different philosophically. That was about avoiding life—this is about living it . . . or what I have *left* of it, at least."

Tim: "What you have left of it? So living life is having me wash dishes and clothes while you look at Facebook?"

Me: "Pretty much."

Tim: "Look, let's not argue. Just wash the dishes and get me some drawers to wear, okay?"

Me: "*You* can say that, your parents are both still alive and they are eighty."

Tim: "Sometimes things skip a generation. My grandpa committed suicide, and he was younger than I am now. So according to your own standards, I was dead a year ago. I would say being a corpse should get me off the hook for washing dishes."

One of the main benefits of reaching middle age is you *do* begin to contemplate your own mortality. You wonder how you will go; you wonder when. You begin to run numbers from time to time, when you lie in bed or stand in line to renew your license at the DMV. You wonder things like "How many more times over my life span will I have to stand in this goddamned DMV line? Well, if I renew it every four years, and I live four more years . . ."

You wonder at the end of a vacation, when you take a last glance before getting into the hotel shuttle to go home: will I see this place again, or will I die before I get the chance? When you feel you are heading into your godforsaken four-year window, you will start to say good-bye, every time. *Good-bye, Bahamas. Probably won't see you again. Good-bye, Grand Canyon. You are the kind of thing done once a decade, at the most. See ya.* And when this is your habit, you especially *remember* what you just said good-bye to. It stays in your memory, as if it were drawn sadly but beautifully in indelible ink. This is the good part of occasionally contemplating the cancer.

Sometimes you lie awake at night, doing stupid calculations that resemble the work of an insane and hypochondriac actuary. That's just a part of the aging process—you wonder what the score will be; you wonder how it will all play out. When you are very young, you worry about being in a car crash while wearing ugly underwear all the emergency and medical personnel will see. When you get to my age, you don't care if you are wearing a G-string, granny drawers, or Depends Disposable Undergarments. You just want to stick around.

Thank goodness, The Lord, or Horus, or nature, or the universe, or whomever or whatever you may believe in balances this awareness of mortality with a sense of awe and appreciation. Roundabout my age, you start to see more and more people in the obituaries who aren't much older than you are. You know you better spend your years wisely, either in roller-skating, or in telling your friends what you really think, or in drinking Cherry Cokes. Sometimes you are glad to be alive, glad to still have legs for roller-skating. You are glad to have a few friends and that you don't yet have cataracts.

Sometimes you even consider, for a brief fleeting moment, that the marks of age—the wrinkles, the sunspots, the gray hairs—are not bad things, but are actually badges of good luck, cosmetic damages that my mother never had the good fortune to grow old with. She saw one clambake too few and unfortunately died suspended in that midpoint between young and old. She died at an age that wasn't young enough to seem eternal, like a James Dean or a Marilyn. But it is also not *old* enough for your loss to seem the natural order of things. Maybe this means that when they really kick in full-force, I should welcome some wrinkles with grace. Perhaps having lots of them means I have made it.

There are many upsides to a midlife crisis, believe it or not. One of them is that you may begin to see things through a different prism, which patiently waits for you on the other side of the hill. It is a prism that makes you say, "The cancer has not gotten me yet!"

Can you think of anything more joyful?

21

An Eternal Sunshine
of the Midlife Mind

"How old would you be if you didn't know how old you were?"
—Satchel Paige

We often played on the sidewalks that lined our neighborhood streets. A segment of this pavement ran in front of our home when I was growing up, and served as a stolid and reliable connector between us kids and the outside world. Without it, we were doomed to isolation in the yard; leaving the sidewalk and stepping off into the city streets was off limits.

This narrow channel of concrete, every bump and groove of which I have so memorized that I could no doubt sketch for you today, served as our playground. It started near our house, running past those two empty lots that were always filled with weeds and makeshift cardboard clubhouses. It ran by us, then on past Mrs. Kathy's house, past Mr. Ray's, and on down in the direction of Lake Pontchartrain, with its raised levee in the distance.

We were told never to go farther than the white house down by the corner. Surely our parents knew some pervs must have lived past the white house, just waiting to get at us in our tube socks and short shorts and T-shirts showing *Star Wars* or Holly Hobbie or the Legion of Doom.

My siblings were usually there on the sidewalk with me. There were my two sisters—my roommates and constant companions—and a little brother toddling around us, watching. Back when we were kids, children actually lolled away their summer afternoons in the yard or on the playground. All summer and every afternoon during the school year we fooled around and teased each other and ate makeshift Kool-Aid cones we called icees that neighborhood moms had frozen in paper Dixie cups. We knocked on doors looking for playmates and had no more to worry about than a simple directive: be home by supper.

Kids did this in complete ignorance of what was to come in the future. They didn't know they were missing out on the advanced hand-eye coordination that kids of today would pick up while sitting drooling in front of video games. They also didn't know of the true bonding that would happen between the kids of the future when they texted each other saying important and eloquent things, such as: "R U bored?"

Back in our childish ignorance, before "useful" technology, we would often ride bicycles, the kind with streamers dangling from the end of the handlebars and a plastic white basket on front, adorned with colorful flowers. Sometimes we would draw crooked, chalky hopscotches and use smooth rocks or pennies as the game markers we would toss carefully so they would land smack-dab on the right square. Occasionally, a gang of innocent boys needing warm bodies would drag us gently from the sidewalk into the grass for a game of tackle football. We girls served as filler when there were unevenly populated teams; they always had to wait while we went inside to put on a pair of shorts under our skirts.

On a particular day one summer, however, we did my very favorite thing. We roller-skated. This was during a period that was sort of transitional for roller-skate technology. When I first learned to skate, at age four or five, roller skates had been a clunky and inaccurate affair—they were shiny metal things that were held on to the bottom of tennis shoes with leather straps. You could make them larger or smaller by pulling the heel section and the toe section apart and lengthening the sliding metal bar that supported the arch of the foot. The wheels wobbled and clanked, and after a few uses the metal became so scratched and rutted that they made this awful abrasive sound when used.

But by my ninth or tenth year, roller-skate technology had propelled itself forward. Now, like the ones you could rent in the rinks with fancy rubber wheels, most store-bought skates consisted of a heavy leather shoe. Most still had metal wheels, but they were attached firmly. It wasn't yet perfect, but was much, much better.

This is the kind of skate I had. The metal was some sort of shiny aluminum. It made a loud damn racket on the sidewalk when we skated. No doubt this use of such noisy materials was a strategy of the roller-skate industry to curb juvenile delinquency. When things suddenly grew quiet outside, parents would know that the skating had stopped and that trouble was, indeed, brewing.

So I was there on this summer afternoon, and my sisters had stopped skating and had left home to run errands with my mother and little brother. I played outside. Even with the skates on, I was out of earshot of our live-in grandmother, who was supposed to be supervising. She had her "soaps" turned up so loud she couldn't hear my skates' clank, thus diminishing their effectiveness in curbing juvenile delinquency.

This was unfortunate for my Gran. She was a funny kind of grandmother. She told jokes and took out her fake teeth to make faces that looked like a pig. Sometimes she would raise her hand up to us as if to strike and would make some kind of idle threat that never, ever came to pass. She had been pretty freewheeling as a parent and now, as a grandparent, was downright cool. She was the kind of grandmother who would call out from her seat in the recliner, "What are you doing? Is everything okay?"

And one of us, or all of us, would likely say something like "Oh, we're just trying to light a few things on fire in here, everything is fine." Or, "We are spraying a Waterpik into the back of a hairdryer, just to see if it will mist water on us!" or some such thing.

She would always go back to watching *As the World Turns* or *Wheel of Fortune*, satisfied all was well since somebody actually answered her inquiry.

On this day Gran was probably inside pondering the fate of J.R. Ewing ("Who shot him? *Who?*"), or some such thing, while I enjoyed the time alone outside. I skated. I made grand dashes down the sidewalk in an attempt to break the sound barrier with my speed. I put every muscle into it, every fiber. I started down near the empty lots, past our house, past Mrs. Kathy's invasive Chinese tallow tree. I sped by Mr. Ray's and the fire hydrant and past that disabled kid's house and on to the end, at the very edge of where the pervs must live. I came back. I did the same thing, again. Sweat flung to my sides as I skated, body salt christening the air. I jumped the familiar bumps in the sidewalk. I got control when I would start to go a little too fast on a smooth area of concrete, or when I would start some kind of wild, unexpected career. I never tired of that feeling of gliding on eight wheels, a little bit in control, a little bit not.

Sometimes I wonder if my feelings about skating are distant echoes of my attitudes toward life in general, now. I am a little bit in control, a little bit not. But on this particular summer day, there was not even a little bit of control to be had. I relinquished that to someone who was the color of a sunset.

His name was Sunshine. He was orange-ish red. He had scratchy, wiry fur that, in retrospect, was not all that fun to rub. A good old mutt, he was a near-feral yard dog that was our family pet. He smelled pretty bad. He seemed to always want to get it on but was unable to, since our yard contained no lady friends (unless, of course, you include the legs of visitors). He scratched incessantly at the sliding-glass door to our backyard that separated him from our family life. He was isolated. When he wasn't scratching, he was patiently watching us, kind of like in that made-for-TV movie with John Travolta, *The Boy in the Plastic Bubble*. Only he wasn't a boy, and his bubble was a small suburban yard filled with chaise lounges and swing sets and rusty trikes. He was always ready to rumble.

Of course Sunshine chooses the day I am skating alone while my grandmother inside pretends to babysit as his day to sow some wild canine oats. The whole while that I am peacefully gliding and clanking my aluminum, jumping sidewalk bumps and imagining lifting off and taking flight, he is simply digging for dear life. He is tunneling under our wooden fence in an escape from his own personal Alcatraz:

The DogMind of Sunshine: "Dig, dig, dig, don't stop digging! That old bat inside ain't watching and most of the pack is shopping at Sears! Now's your chance, old boy! Do they think I wanna watch them from behind glass the rest of my life when there are butts out there to sniff? Dig . . . dig . . . dig . . . good boy . . ."

No doubt he tells himself this.

Eventually, he moves earth like a crazed canine backhoe to burrow a slim passageway wide enough to wiggle into and through to the other side.

The DogMind of Sunshine: "Holy crap, you made it! You're out! Gotta get a lady friend . . . gotta get a lady friend . . . believe in yourself, you old dawg, you can do it . . .you're *free!*"

So Sunshine runs, frenetically, passionately. He sniffs the St. Augustine grass and the hedge and the base of the mailbox. He sniffs some rocks where a frog once decomposed and he takes a very quick pee. He lingers over a dirty garbage pail and feels, really and truly, that *this is the life!* And then . . . he hears something.

The DogMind of Sunshine: "What the hell is that sound? Sounds like cheap aluminum roller skates. It's deafening! Better look back there . . . oh my God, they are being worn by that girl, the one who always teases me and waves around hot dogs from behind the glass. *Run, Sunshine, run!*"

Out of the corner of my eye, I spy the beloved yet isolated Sunshine darting off around the corner. Based on past experience, I understand full well that he won't return of his own volition. It is all but certain he won't come back. I know if I were to run inside and tell her what had happened, Gran would make some kinda pig face and just say: "Dog? What dog? Now be quiet and go play, I am watching Ronnie Reagan's big scene."

So what did I do? I chased him around, for hour upon hour. When he sprints, I roll faster. When he rests, I approach more quietly in the mistaken notion that he will allow me to pounce and take hold of his raggedy brown collar. Every time I lean in for a grab, he darts off again in search of his first successful mount.

I can remember thinking, even at the time, I felt sorry for old Sunshine. I had a split allegiance to both the notion that he should be kept in the yard and the idea that he should run free. I thought of the phrase that seemed to be ubiquitous in the late '70s and early '80s, and that, in fact, appeared on a poster of a butterfly that once hung on my wall:

"If you love something, set it free. If it comes back, it's yours. If not, it was never meant to be."

Could Sunshine be like this butterfly in the poster? Would he come back so I could taunt him through the glass again with a salty Vienna sausage or bit of pepperoni?

I chased him through tears, my heart pounding such that it hurt. My feet had blisters. My face was sunburned. But I knew full well that losing sight of him meant losing him forever. He would never, ever choose to come back.

And I wonder now, looking back on it all, if somehow these recent days and months—these turning-into-years—of midlife hysteria have found me again in a sort of roller derby pursuit that resembles childhood. Am I like I was on that day when I was just nine, simply chasing an unstoppable tail? Am I somehow chasing the little *me*, who dangled hot dogs like unattainable carrots and flew down sidewalks like a bird, plastic streamers waving behind my handlebars? Am I chasing, in fits and starts composed of cell phones and music players and makeovers and uke-harp groups and rock concerts and drunken prances and performance art and new pairs of shoes—am I chasing, over curbs and sidewalk cracks, and in clompings over the grass of vacant lots, *something that wants to move on*?

I don't have an answer to this question, much as there was no answer to the Sunshine dilemma on that summer day. I didn't know if I was trying to snag something that wanted only to avoid capture, or that simply was not meant to be. All I knew is that he ran, as that little girl is running now, into the distance. All I could do then is what I do now, at the inception of middle age: engage the chase.

On that day long ago I actually feared I would die, or Sunshine would, before one of us relented. I really did. My heart pounded so hard from sadness, fear, and dehydration, I thought it would rupture. I thought I would eventually fall down with weird chills, passed out from the heat stroke my worrywart mother had always said would come if we stayed out too long during hot months. My imagination mapped out scenarios where strangers would chance upon me lying there, on a suburban New Orleans sidewalk, and not have a clue what had happened:

Innocent Bystander A: "Hey, look at this. What's wrong with her? Is she dead?"

Innocent Bystander B: "I think so. But why is she wearing roller skates?"

Innocent Bystander A: "I don't know, but a better question is—why is that mangy dog mounting one of them?"

Through all of my imaginings, though, never once did it occur to me to see the chase through the eyes of the frightened animal.

The DogMind of Sunshine: "I am so sick of that noise. What the hell is that racket? Sounds a little like thunder! Since I'm not finding any lady friends, *I would sure love to go back home and sit in the sun*. If only that girl would stop following me with that noise! *Run, Sunshine, run!*"

I didn't know the sound of my skates is what made him run. It just never crossed my mind.

Eventually I saw the sky begin to glow as a sunset inched itself down behind the horizon. It was the same color as the tired animal I pursued. It was time for the chase to end. We were close to home, but because of pervs it was not safe to be out after dark. I knew I had to let the mutt go. I stopped cold.

It was within seconds of making this decision that the miracle happened.

"Sunshine! Here, boy!" It was my older sister, standing less than a half block from us, exiting the car in our driveway as the rest of my family returned from shopping.

And Sunshine, that old dog, gladly high-tailed it in the direction of home and within seconds jumped right into her arms.

He never did get laid. He never even sniffed any rear ends, despite a noble effort. He came home willingly, when the chase had finally ended. He came home when he was tired, and for no other reason than that he was ready for it to be done.

I wonder if a so-called midlife crisis isn't really just like Sunshine's great run. I wonder if it isn't simply a wanting to be free of the constraints of maturity and bland routine *just to prove that you can.* Just to sniff a last butt or two, just to put on size-six jeans and to trick-or-treat and to try to go back in time and remember every single second of the day you met your husband. Maybe the run is just to prove if you wanted to, you could go back and do all of those things again, only this time do them *right.*

And it's weird, because at the same time that I am saying all of this, I also wonder if the whole while that I am running, into the wilderness and backward up a downward hill, I am somehow still wishing only to go back to that comfortable place on the suburban patio, or to that warm place in the sun, where the grass is matted down just so. Maybe the whole time I am running I realize I am tired, and honestly want to go back home.

It is curious to wonder whether all this analysis has taught us anything we can use. I sure hope my guidance, or misguidance, has at least partially—in a teeny, tiny way—saved your life.

I wonder if you will take things to heart. I wonder if you will wear glitter over your wrinkled and saggy boobs, or remember anything at all about *If you love something, set it free . . .* once you put down this book. I wonder if you can now let your worries take flight like monarchs, migrating.

As for me, no doubt I will continue to consider what it means to grow. How could I not? Maybe growing older will turn out to be a little like Sunshine's return. Maybe, just maybe, it will turn out to be nothing more than a permanent going back behind the glass. And a pant of relief. And a cold lick of water. And a favorite warm spot in the sun.

But this returning has to be done freely. It cannot happen under the demands of time, or on some schedule that is marked up by stupid charts and graphs monitoring crow's-feet and counts of gray hairs. It has to happen without worrying, and after letting go of the need to prove anything to yourself, or to anyone else.

We must end it by quietly jumping off the pavement and into the arms of someone we love, instead of under the stress of a metallic, clanging chase.

Index

ABOUT THE AUTHOR

Kara Martinez Bachman is a New Orleans-based freelance writer. Her work has appeared in the *New Orleans Times-Picayune*, NOLA.com, *The Writer*, *Funny Times*, NPR's *State of the Re:Union*, *Ellipsis*, *Magnolia Quarterly*, the ten-year anniversary of Hurricane Katrina retrospective *Katrina Memoirs*, and numerous other publications.

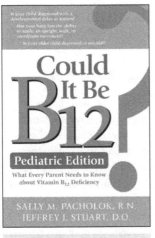

Calming adult coloring books from Quill Driver Books

$14.95 ($18.95 Canada)

Elegant Tea Party Coloring Book
You're Invited ... Relax and Enjoy!
Illustrated by Laurie Triefeldt

Sit down, have a cup, ease your tensions, and reinvigorate your creativity in the immersive world of the ***Elegant Tea Party Coloring Book***. Hand-drawn by acclaimed artist Laurie Trifeldt, these 70 intricate and absorbing illustrations of cups, saucers, teapots, muffins, and flowers will give you hours of calming focus. Thick, high-quality paper, printed on only one side, gives you a firm coloring surface, and perforated pages let you share and preserve your work. Like a rich cup of tea, this is a relaxing and stimulating break in your busy day.

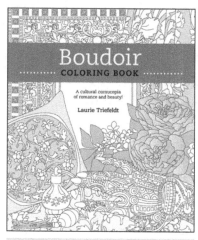

$14.95 ($18.95 Canada)

Boudoir Coloring Book
A cultural cornucopia of romance and beauty!
Illustrated by Laurie Triefeldt

Every coloring book fan who loves a touch of feminine glamour and elegance can find their own private place in the enchanting world of ***Boudoir Coloring Book***. These intricate images of elegant ladies, vanity tables, perfume, make up, and flowers will transport colorists to a place of rest and relaxation. Thick, high-quality paper, printed on only one side, gives you a firm coloring surface, and perforated pages let you share and preserve your work. Find your own personal world far away from stress within these enchanting images.

Available from bookstores, online bookstores, and QuillDriverBooks.com, or by calling toll-free 1-800-345-4447.

Books for travel and career from Quill Driver Books

$16.95 ($21.95 Canada)

Walking San Francisco's 49 Mile Scenic Drive

Explore the Famous Sites, Neighborhoods, and Vistas in 17 Enchanting Walks
by Kristine Poggioli and Carolyn Eidson

Walking San Francisco's 49 Mile Scenic Drive takes you the length of the famous 49 Mile Drive in 17 bite-size walks, complete with turn-by-turn instructions, maps, and historical facts. Each chapter introduces the must-see sights, landmarks, and secret treasures of a specific San Francisco neighborhood, while leading the reader along a healthy but nonstrenuous urban hike. It's the perfect guidebook for today's urban enthusiast who values walkable neighborhoods, hyperlocal culture, and the pleasure of walking..

$18.95 ($19.95 Canada)

Put College to Work

How to Use College to the Fullest to Discover Your Strengths and Find a Job You Love Before You Graduate
by Kat Clowes, M.B.A.

College graduates face an ever-tougher job market, and a college degree alone won't lead to a career. *Put College to Work* is a supremely practical guide to getting a job you love *before* you graduate. Professional college/career planner Kat Clowes shows how to take advantage of resources available in college to identify your career strengths, network with employers, create your own opportunities, and use college to the fullest to build your career.